Let the Spirit Move You

Let the Spirit Move You

Poetry and Photography
from the Soul

Lynn Noble

Let the Spirit Move You

First Edition December 2015

BeLightFull Books

Thank you WingSpan Press for helping my book to fly.

ISBN 978-0-9968843-0-3

Library of Congress Control Number: 2015916400

This book was conceived, designed, produced and edited by

Lynn Noble
www.lynnnoble.com

This book is dedicated to
all the people, animals and nature in my life,
who have encouraged my
Soul's flame to grow!!!
Thank you!!! ☺

Thank you Spirit… for always being with me!!! ☺

Contents

Passing Storms

Dark to Light

Release

Growth

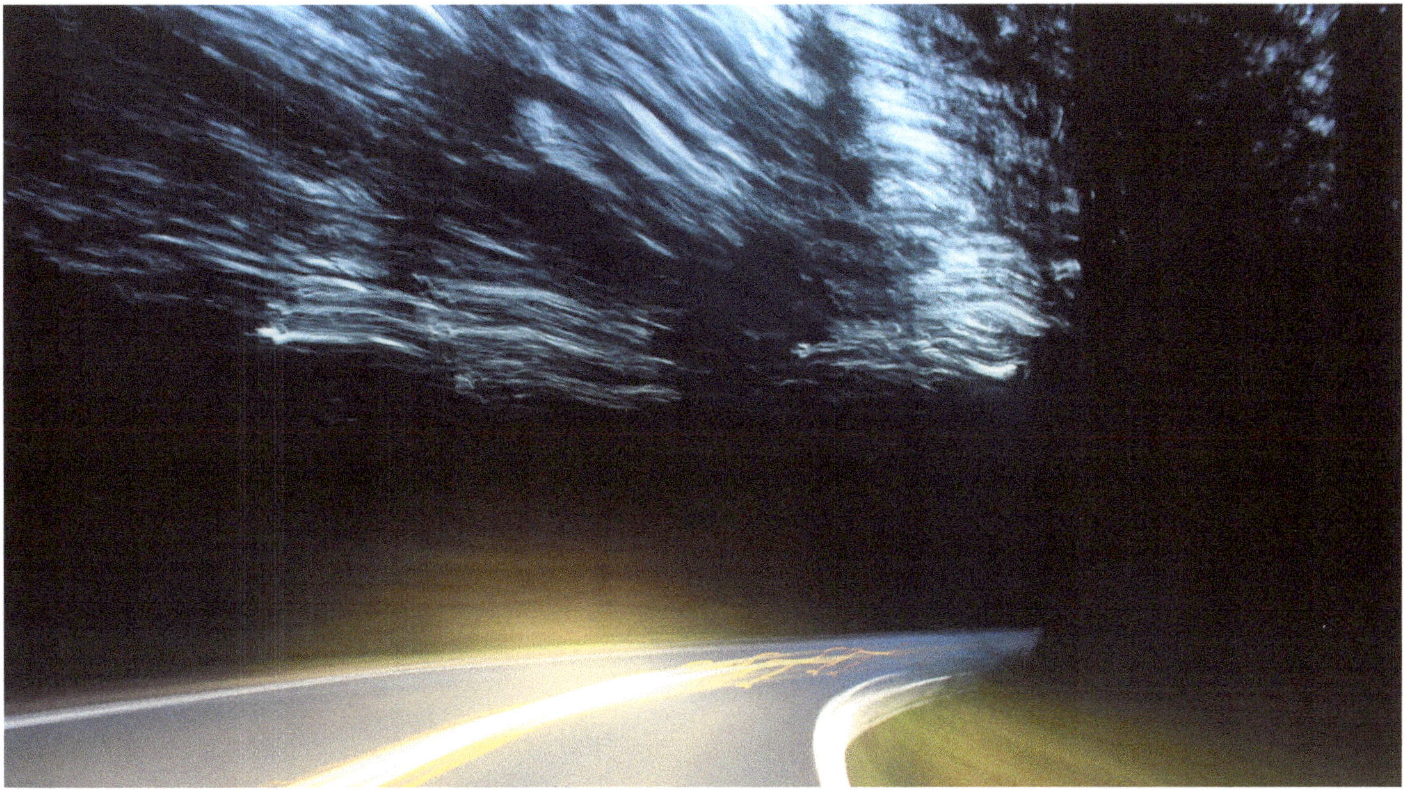

I love capturing "Spirit" in all of my work.
Whether it be photographing dancers and nature, or writing from my Soul…
there is always something to be seen in the unseen.
When I shoot, it is always about being present, feeling the music from within and
letting myself go with the flow as I change my aperture, shutter speed and focal lengths.
There is always a connection to be felt as I capture what is in front of me.
My photos are a moment in time… unchanged by technology.
When I write, it is about being still, quieting my mind and allowing my Soul to be heard.
I honor my messages by keeping them exactly as they come through… unchanged by my mind.

My hope is to inspire everyone along their journey,
to embrace their Spirit from within and let it shine onto others!!! ☺

I am Me… the Beginning of my Spiritual Journey

I am like no other.
I am me.
I am a seeker of truth and perfection…
I find myself waiting until the two become reality.
I am a mother.
I am a good mother and a bad mother.
I am a good listener, yet I don't hear.
I am torn between an amazing driving force, yet I procrastinate.
I can see my life clearly, then I have no direction.
I am at the top of the brightest sky,
I am at the bottom of the darkest sea.
I am like no other.
I am me.
I am black and white. No in-between.
I am… or I am not.

I feel forces guiding me, but I get confused in their message.
What is life?
What is family?
What are we here to do?
Who should we open our life to?
There are so many people, who should we close off?
My Spirit is spread over such a large area,
I need to confine it, to control it.
But it is my Spirit that keeps reaching out to the farthest depths.
All I want is control, but I can't control life…
and that is where my struggle lies.
Is that our purpose?
To try to find our way on a path that is not visible?
Sometimes I feel as if there is no slowing me down,
my path is an open road.
Then suddenly it turns; my search begins again.
I wish to live my life one day at a time, but I can't.

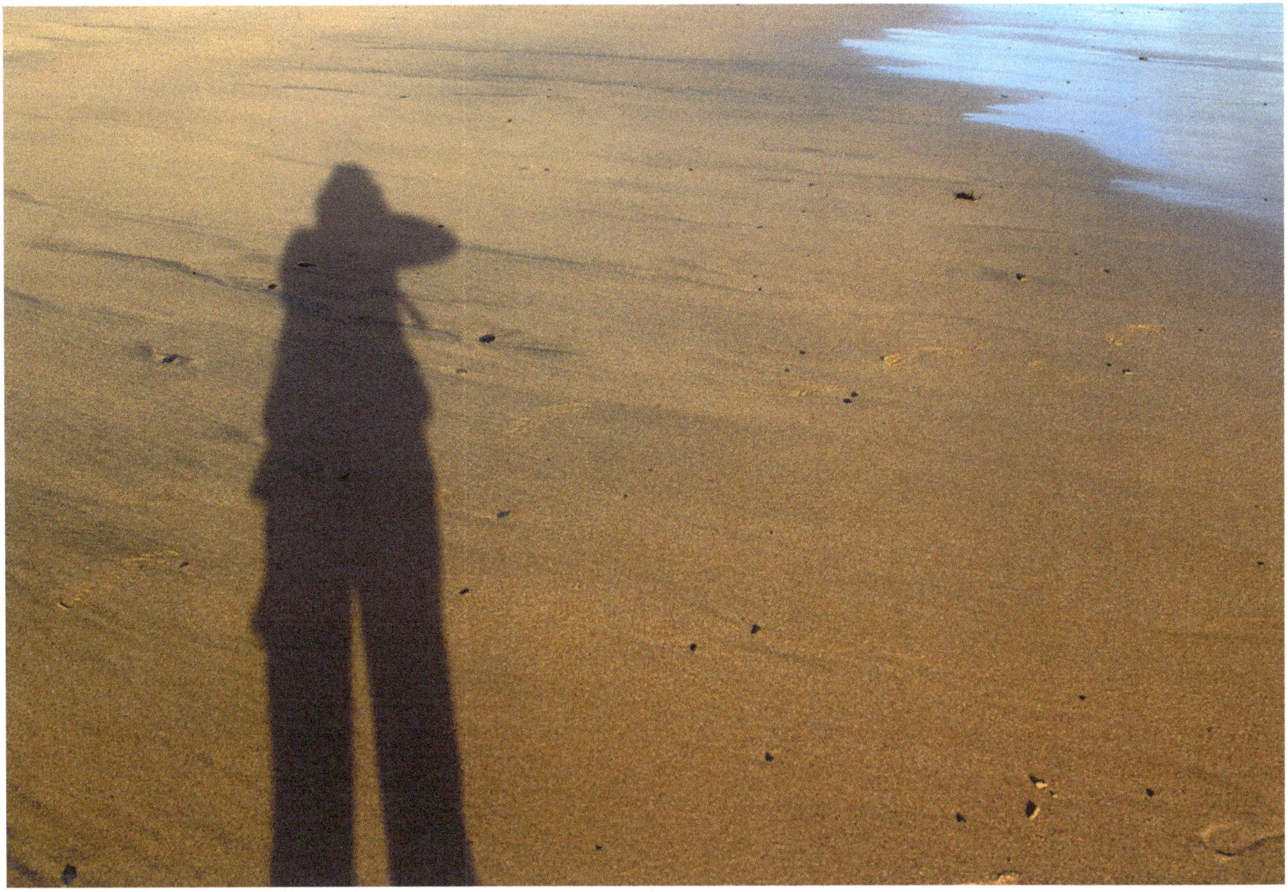

There was a time I strived to be like others.
Now, I strive to be me.
The more I write, the clearer the message.
I want to be me… every part of me… the light and the dark.
I want to feel everything.
Once again, I am like no other.
I am me.
In search of truth and perfection.
I may never find it, but I can say that I tried.
I am me.

Awaken your Soul

Let the Spirit Move You

The sound of your Heart has a rhythm.
It is that rhythm,
that guides your Soul to dance.

When you allow your Heart and Soul
to become one with the music...

your body will follow along and be led
to the great potential that is your destiny.

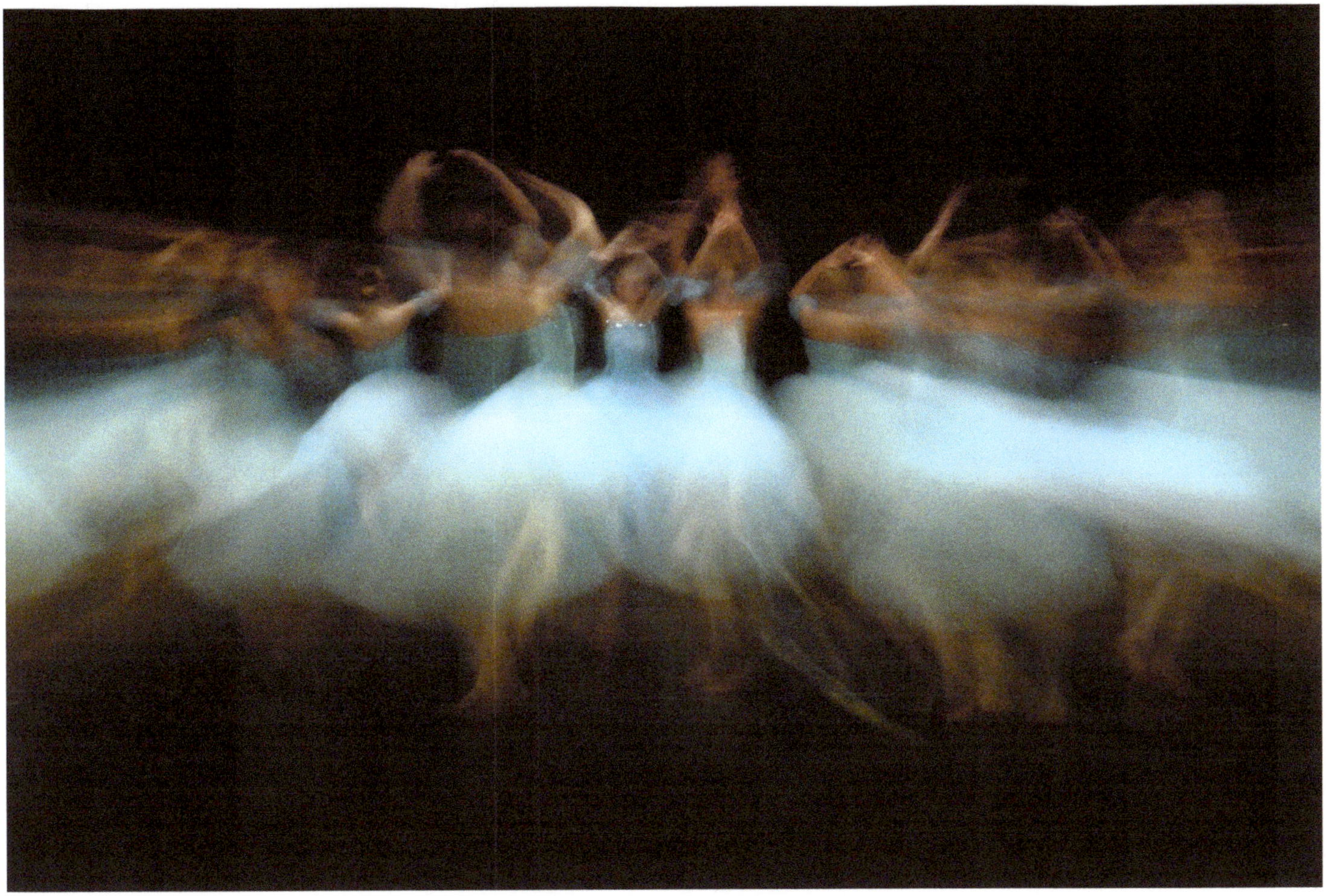

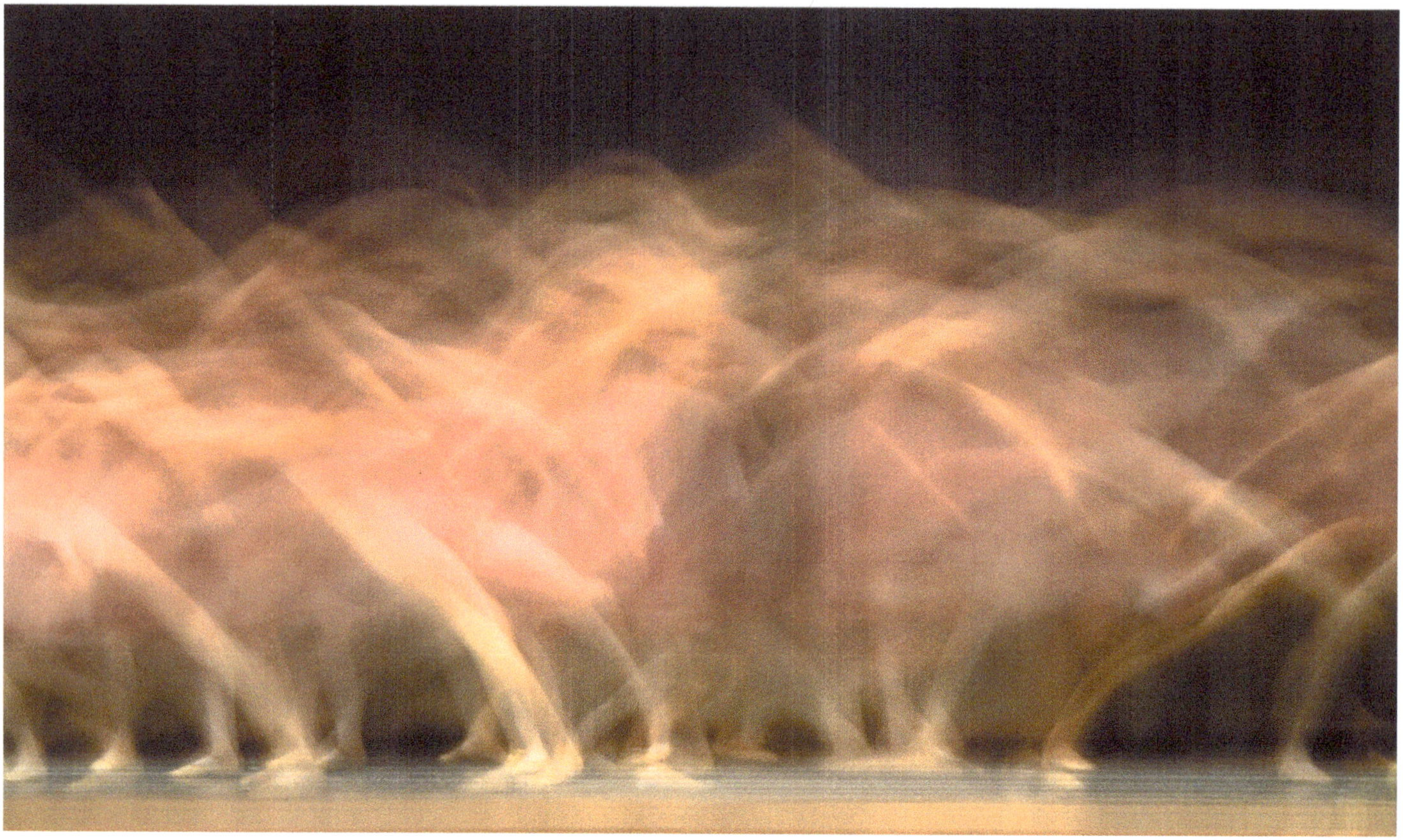

Soul Flame

I watch as the flame from my candle,
dances not to the rhythm of the music...

but to the rhythm that comes from within
and is only felt from the Soul.

The movement is beautiful.

Nourished Life

I watch as the plant that was once limp,
now stands tall and vibrant.

*In life, we all need to know that we can be
nourished by whatever makes our Heart jump.*

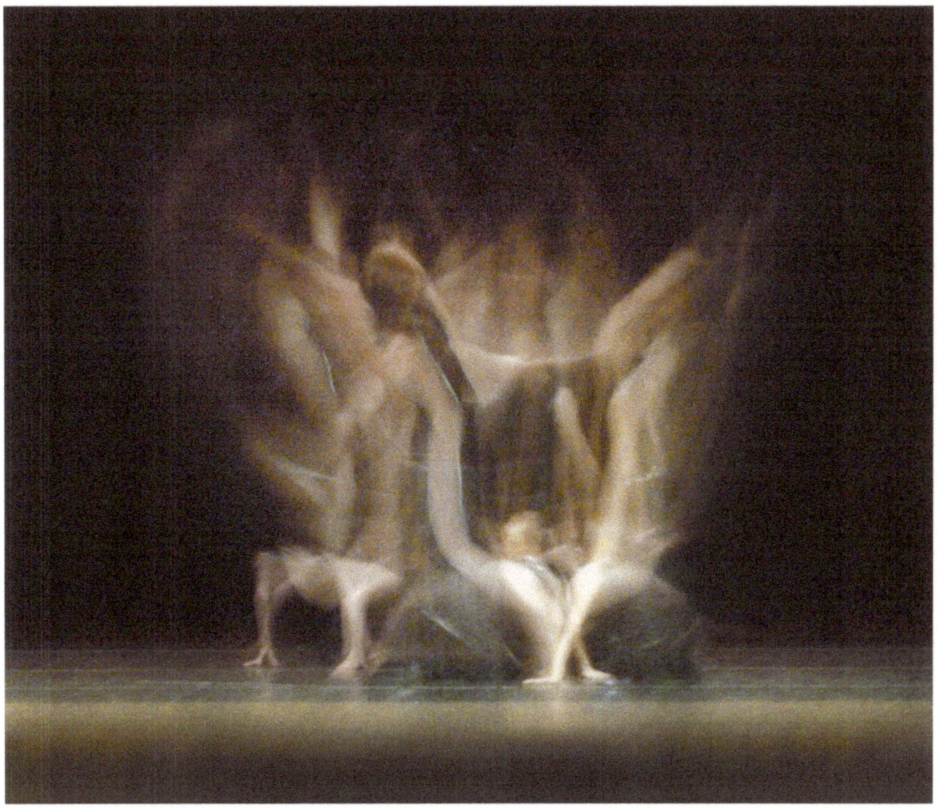

Soul Inside Out

The world around me turns magical,
as I look to the white light of the moon.

Lightning murmurs through the sky
as fireflies flicker in sync with the stars.

The light that dances inside me,
is reflected in all of nature's rhythm.

I know now, what it is like to see my
Soul from the inside out.

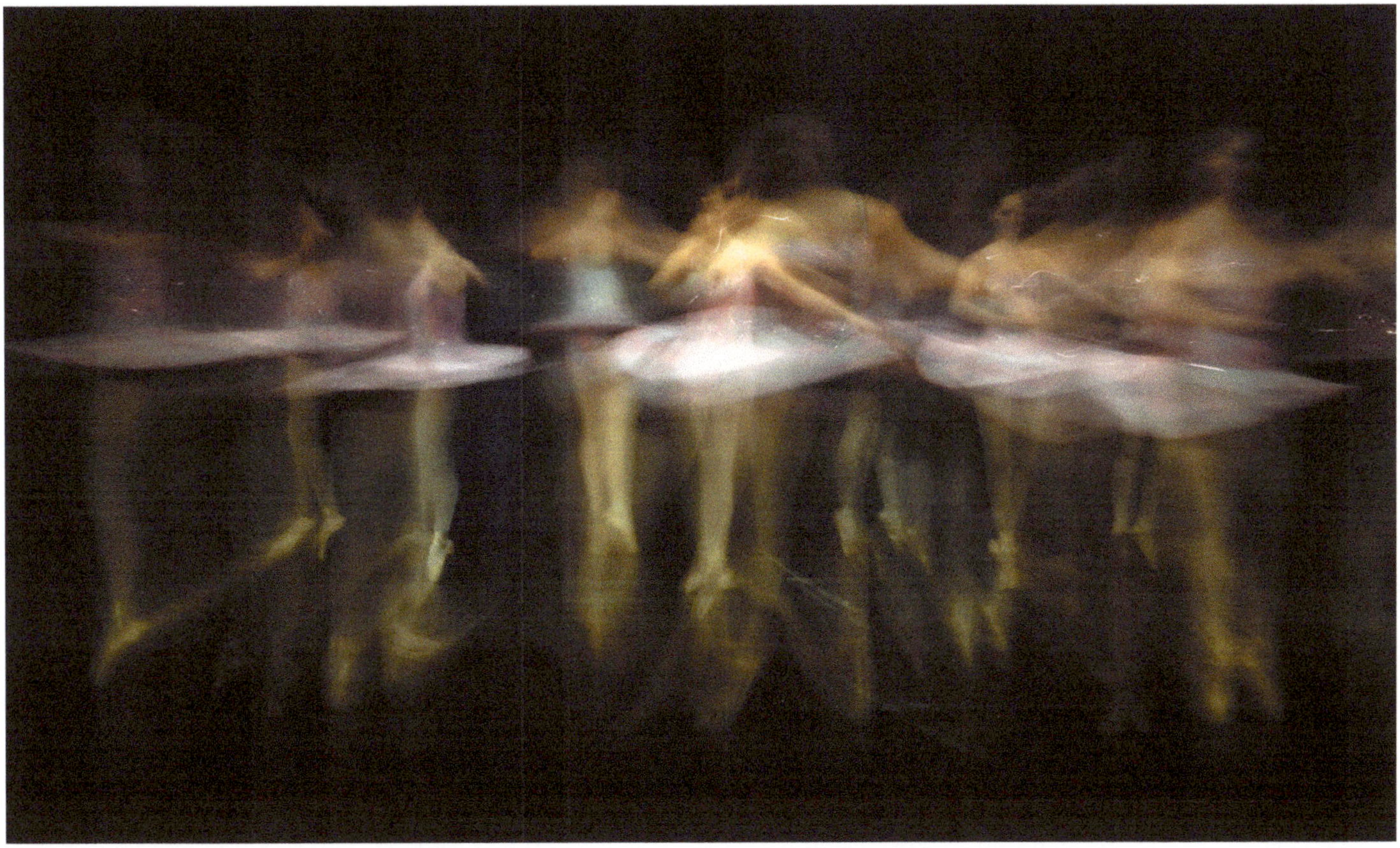

Awaken

As I savor the taste of my favorite
chocolate before bed…

I know that it will awaken me in the
early hours of the morning.

Embrace whatever it is that awakens your Soul.

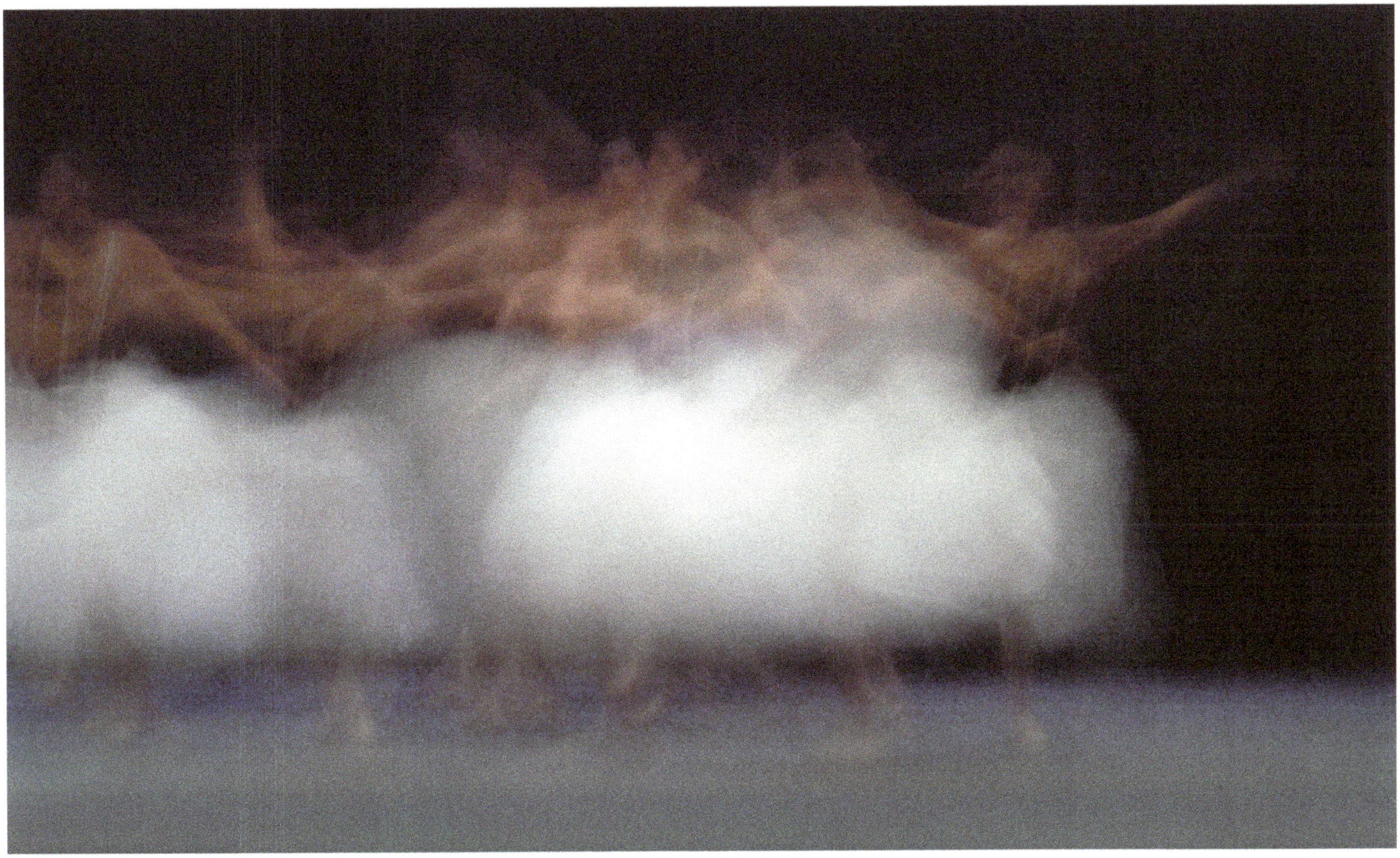

Be a Light

I am Light

I am Light.

When I fully embrace my Light from within,
I feel a warmth and knowing that I am many.

A tear falls as I see myself multiply.

I am surrounded by me...
Pure love.

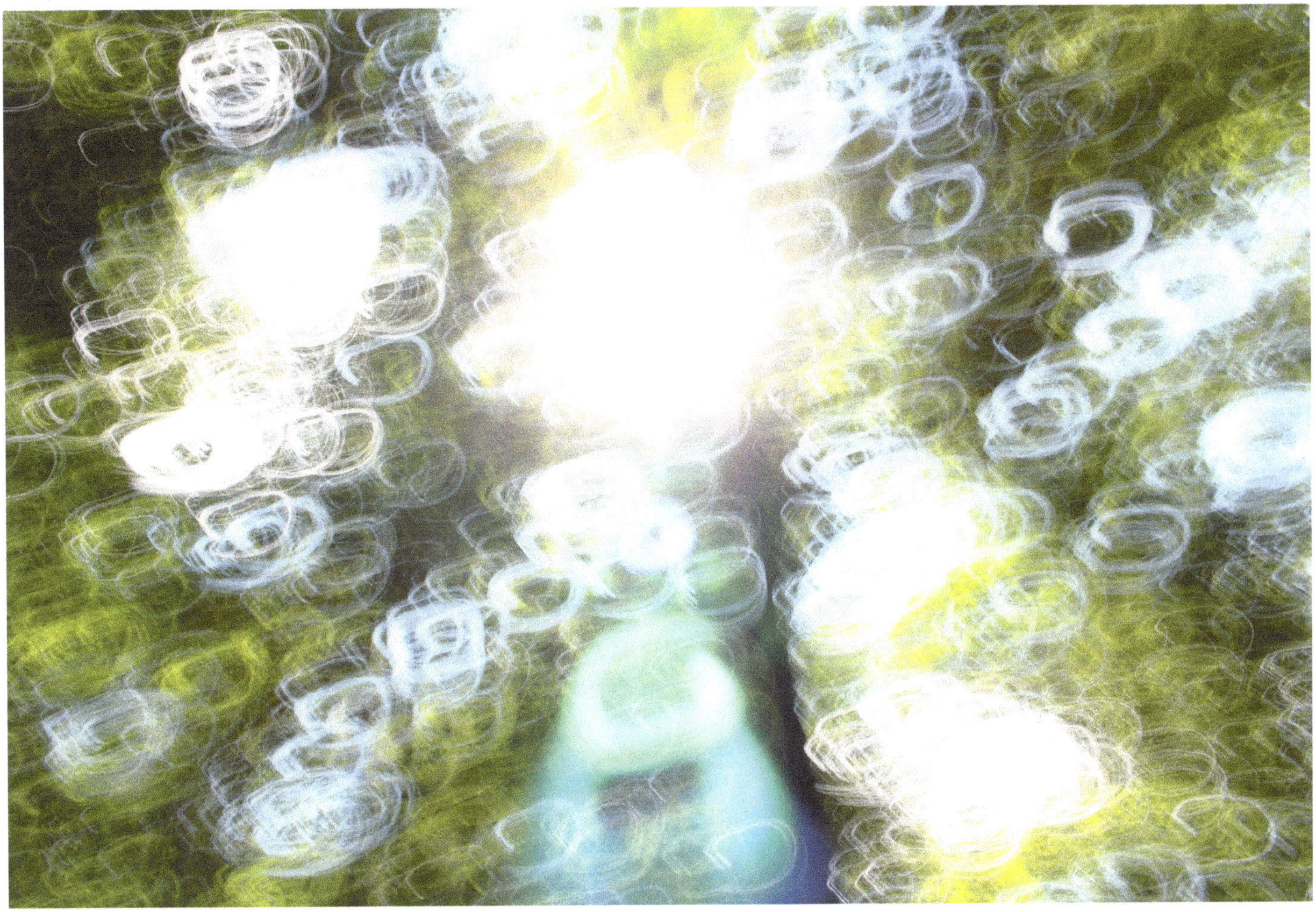

Connecting Souls

We are all Souls that need to connect.

It is that energy that will produce
an amazing light… bright enough,
for even those in the dark to begin to see.

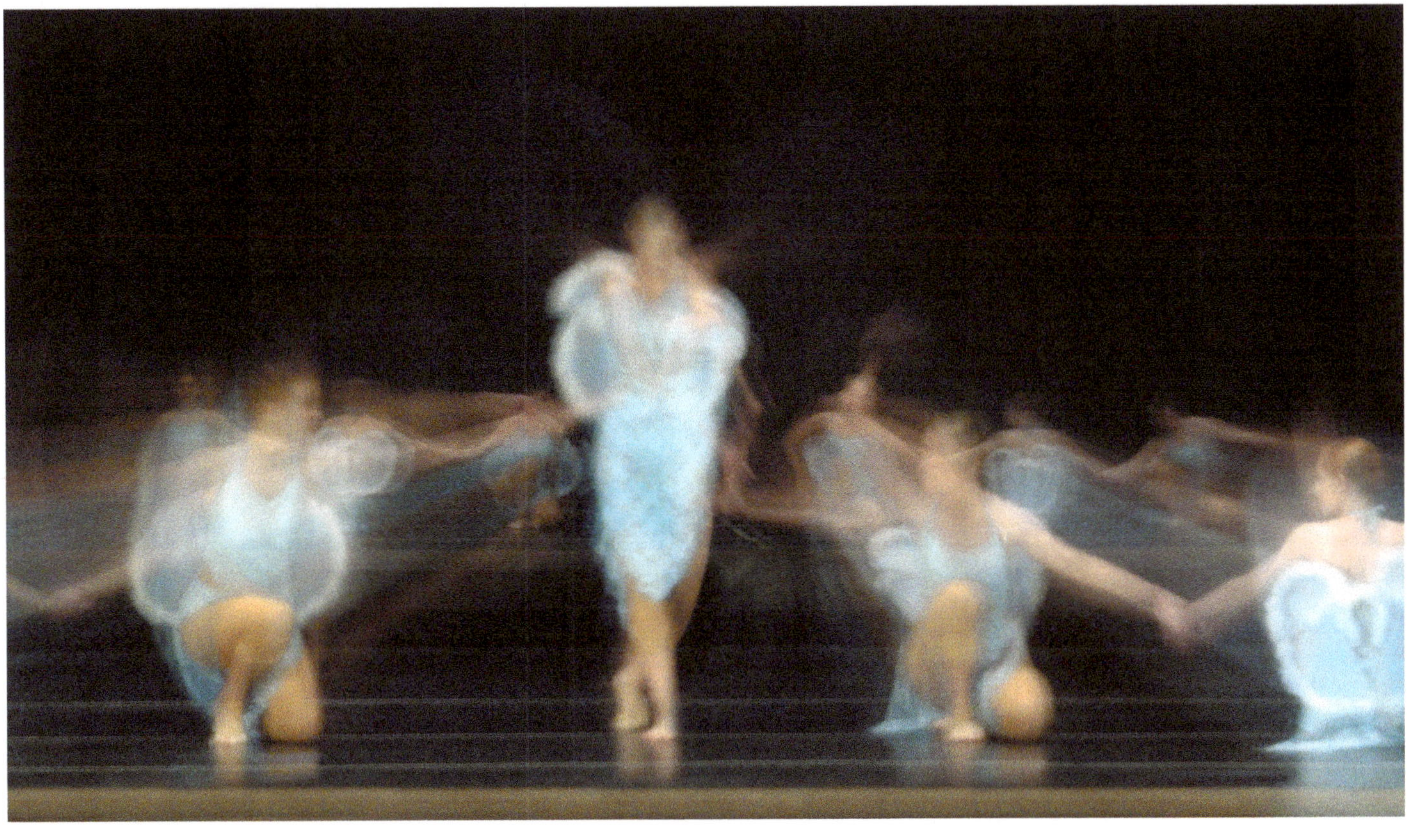

Candlelight

The light from the candle stretches
from side to side, like whiskers on a cat.

Life is like that flame… if you let it shine,
it can light up a whole room.

Be a Light

Staring at the light of the candle…
I realize that life is like this bright light in front of me.

Wherever you are in life, just trust that you too can
project this flame everywhere you go.

People will respond when there is a light from
within someone that they can reach.

All people want that ability to see the light.
It is your responsibility to give them that power.

It is through your stories that people will begin
to understand what it is to have a flame of their own.

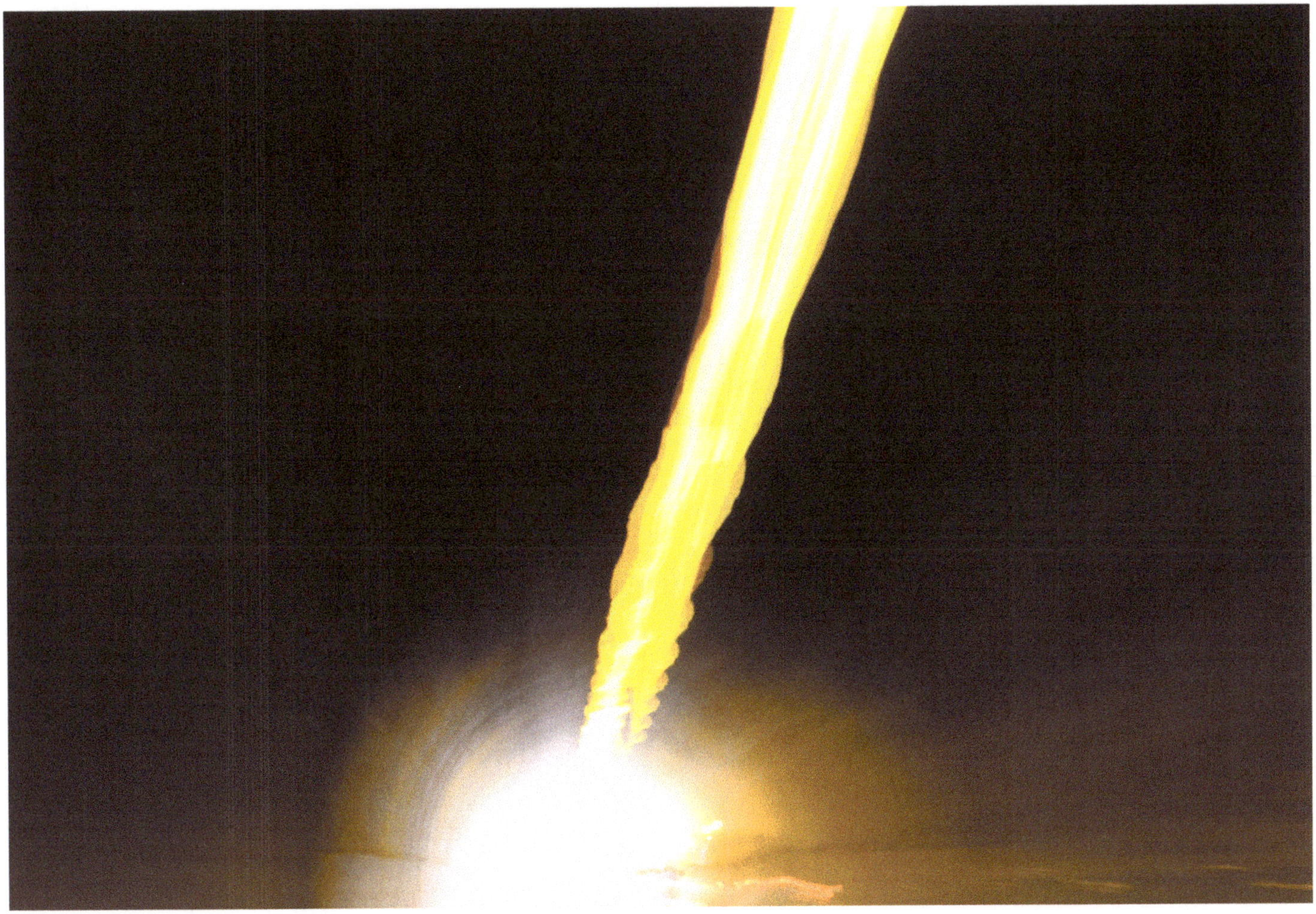

Joy

Life is a sweet joy.

You have so many opportunities
that lie ahead of you…
You are talented beyond belief.

Your joy will carry you far…
You inspire others with your joy.

You are contagious…
People love to be around you.

You bring joy to others…
You have a light that shines far.

Always know that whatever situation
you find yourself in…
your light will shine your way through.

You can never be in darkness.

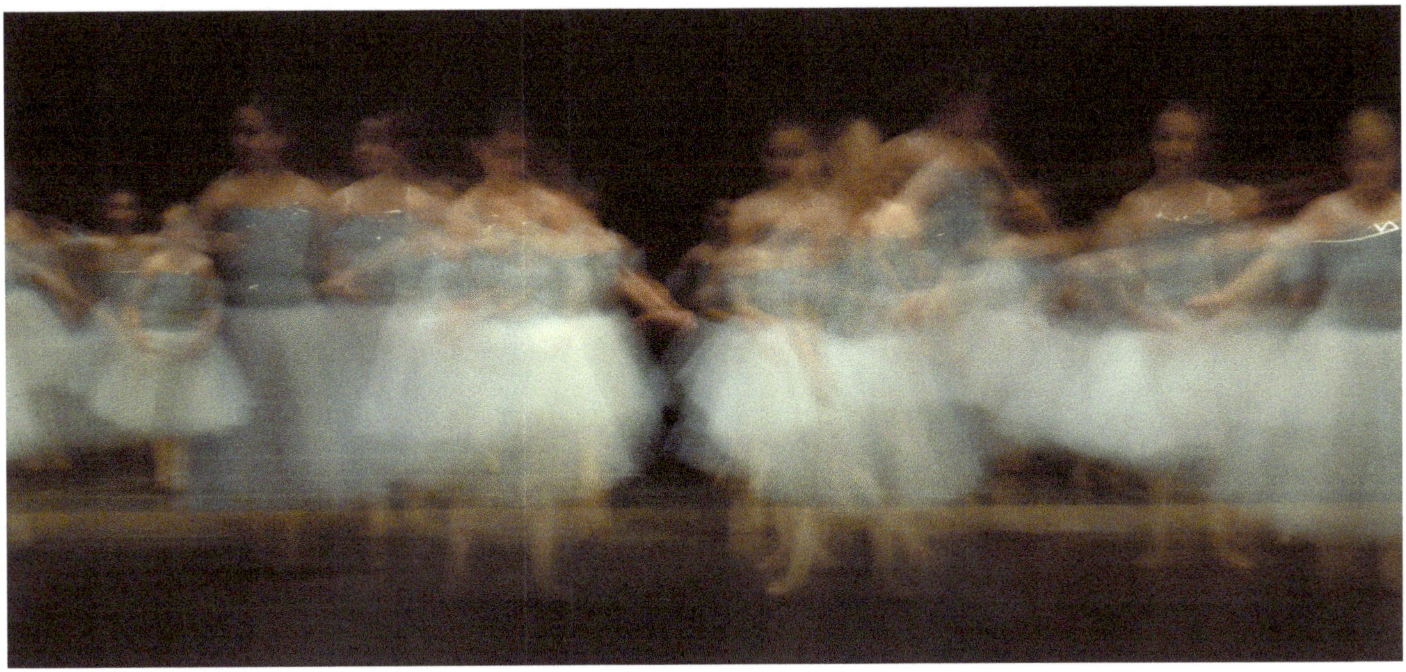

Stillness

Candle's Flame

In stillness…
The flame from my candle
reaches for its higher self.

Slowly it mimics the rhythm
of its surroundings.

It begins to dance wildly as a
passing breeze captures its attention.

It follows along with such intensity…
it forgets to breathe.

The flame stretches far in every direction,
enticed by the excitement.

Little by little…
the flame begins to weaken,
fearful of the dark.

As it breathes in stillness…
once again its light is renewed.

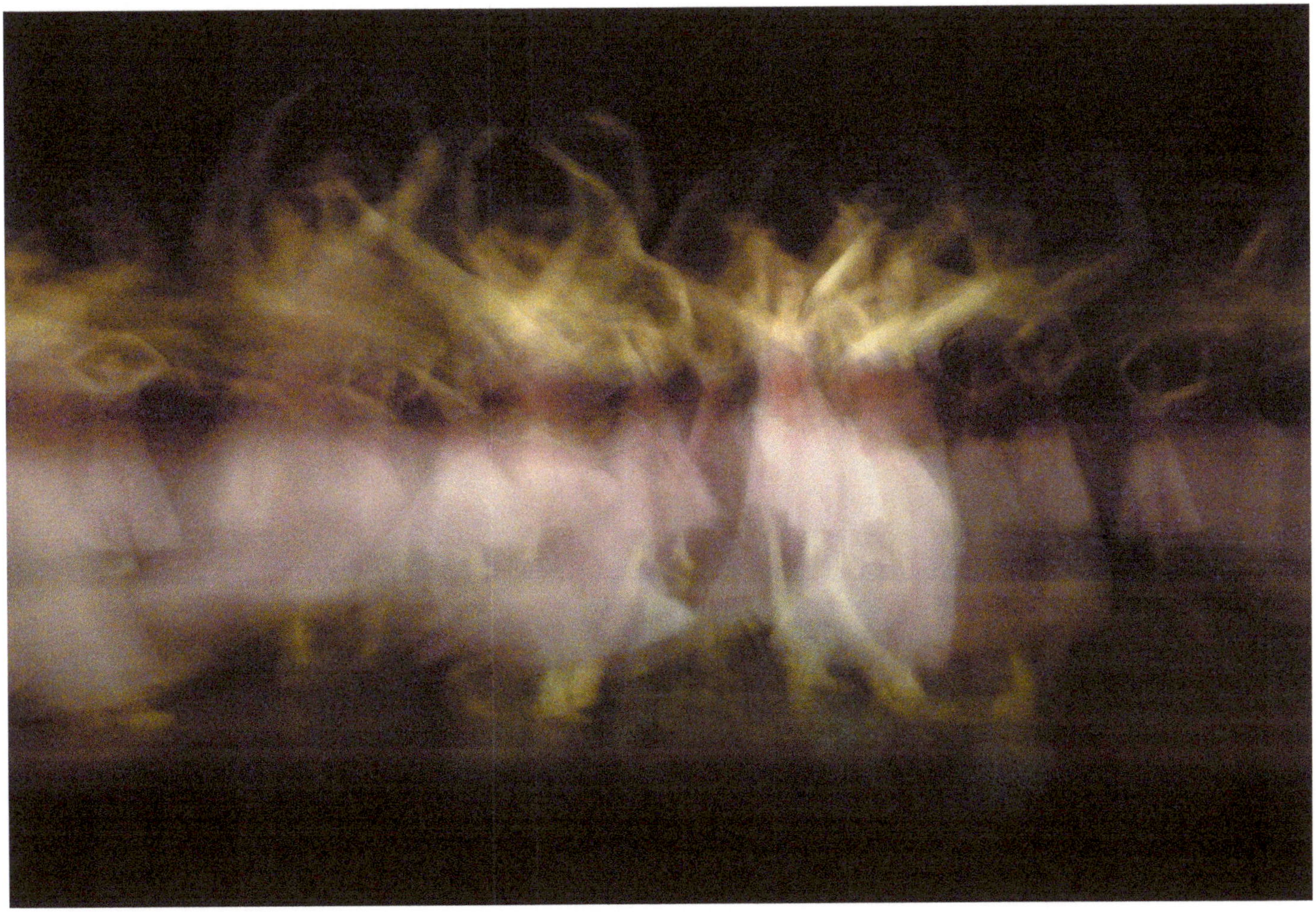

Simplicity of Thought

Stay innocent.

When the mind knows too much,
it will become confused.

Simplicity of thought
will create great gifts.

Trust in the quiet still mind...
Here the greatest truths are found.

Whether it is us or you...
it all holds meaning.

Let go...
Try not to analyze.
Things are as they should be.

Keep it Simple

Life is ever expanding.
It is your life work to keep things simple.

When things are simple...
greater things can be accomplished.

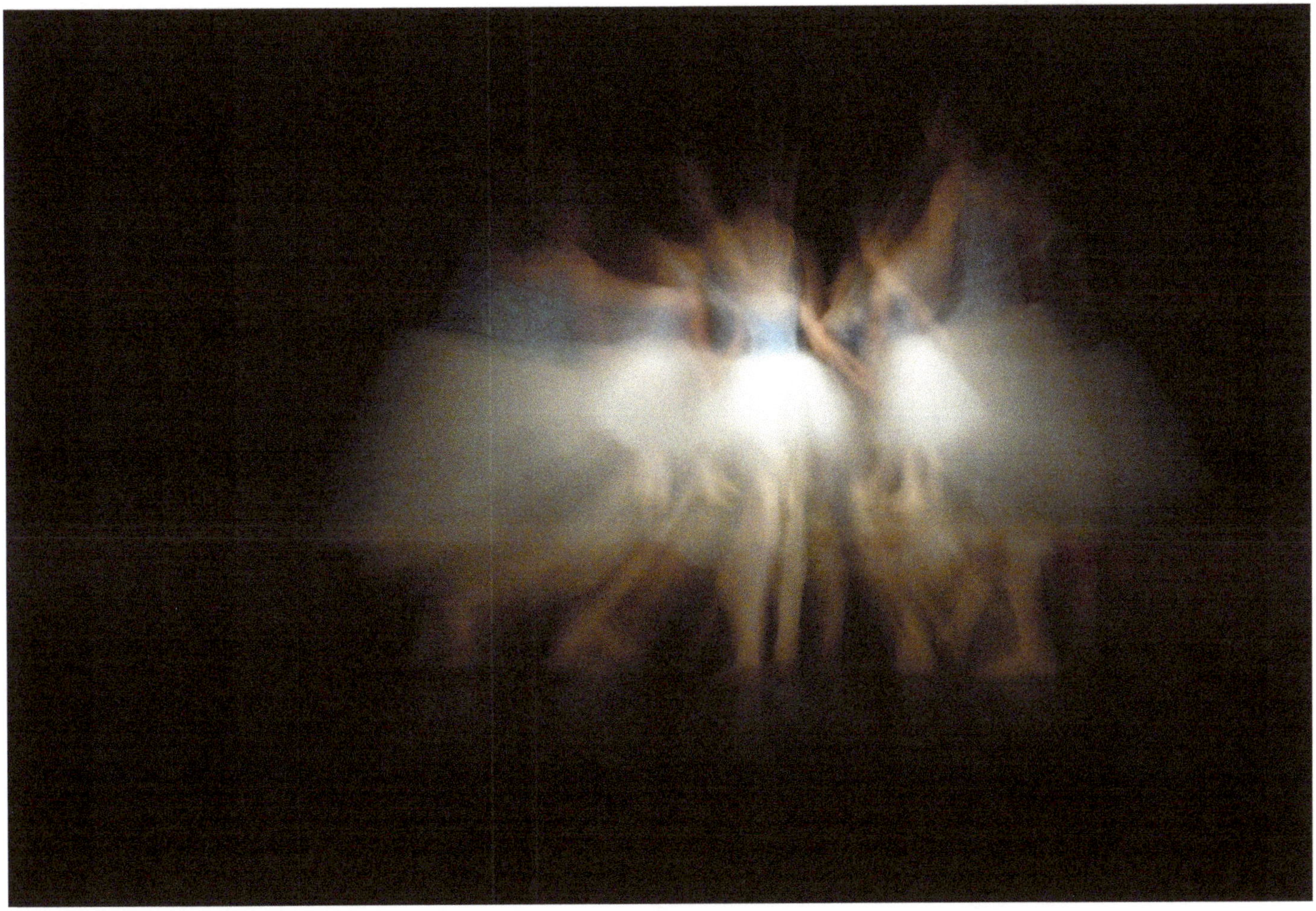

Meditation

My breath is like the flow of the river...
I listen to the sound as it passes through me.

My mind takes its own journey.

As I travel,
I am challenged to find balance.

My Soul grasps at the chance to hold
onto the current, as it twists and turns,
going fast and then slow and then fast again.

The river becomes still like a pond.

It is within this stillness,
that my Soul begins to shine like the sun.

The warmth radiates through my heart
as it is filled with a calm, peaceful understanding.

I feel the river begin to flow once again
through my breath.

It pulls me back.

As I journey home... I know I am not alone.

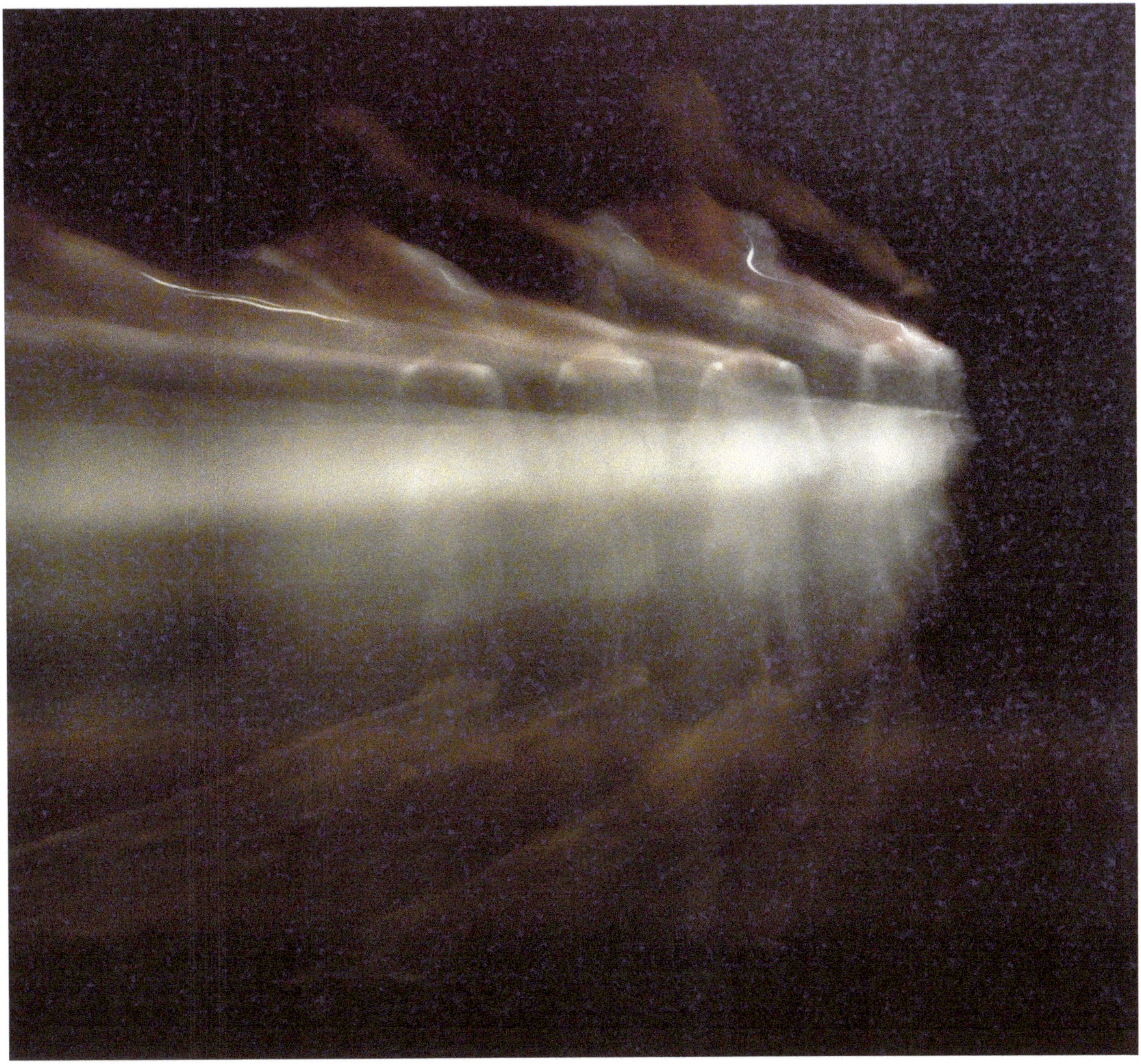

One with Yourself

How do I break free from the
quiet place in my Soul,
when the outside world is calling?

My Soul pleads with me to stay.

I want to stay.
Why should I leave?
Do I have to leave?

Is it possible to be fully in my Soul
while stepping into life?

You will always find the opportunity
to unite the Soul with your mind and body.

Just know you are always one.
You do not have to separate.

That is when life gets beautiful...
When you are one with yourself.

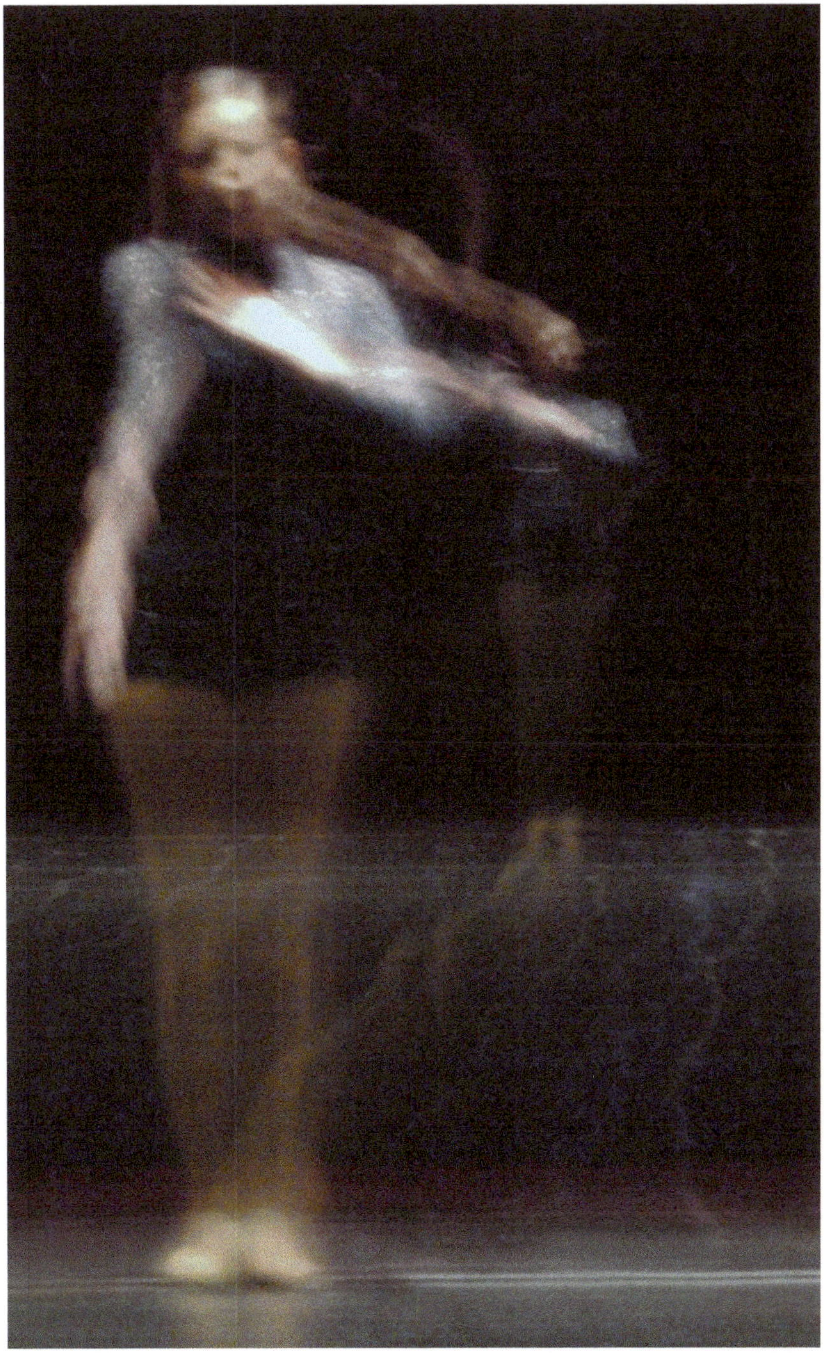

Flow with Ease

Know that when things flow with ease,
you are always on track.

The moment they start to become hard,
you have lost your path.

When we take thinking out of the equation,
we are left with all that is great.

Slow down…
The pace of living is not
always what you think it should be.

Listen to your body…
It will tell you what your pace is.

You need to strip down your life to
wanting nothing except to be happy.

It is only then,
that you will begin to find your purpose.

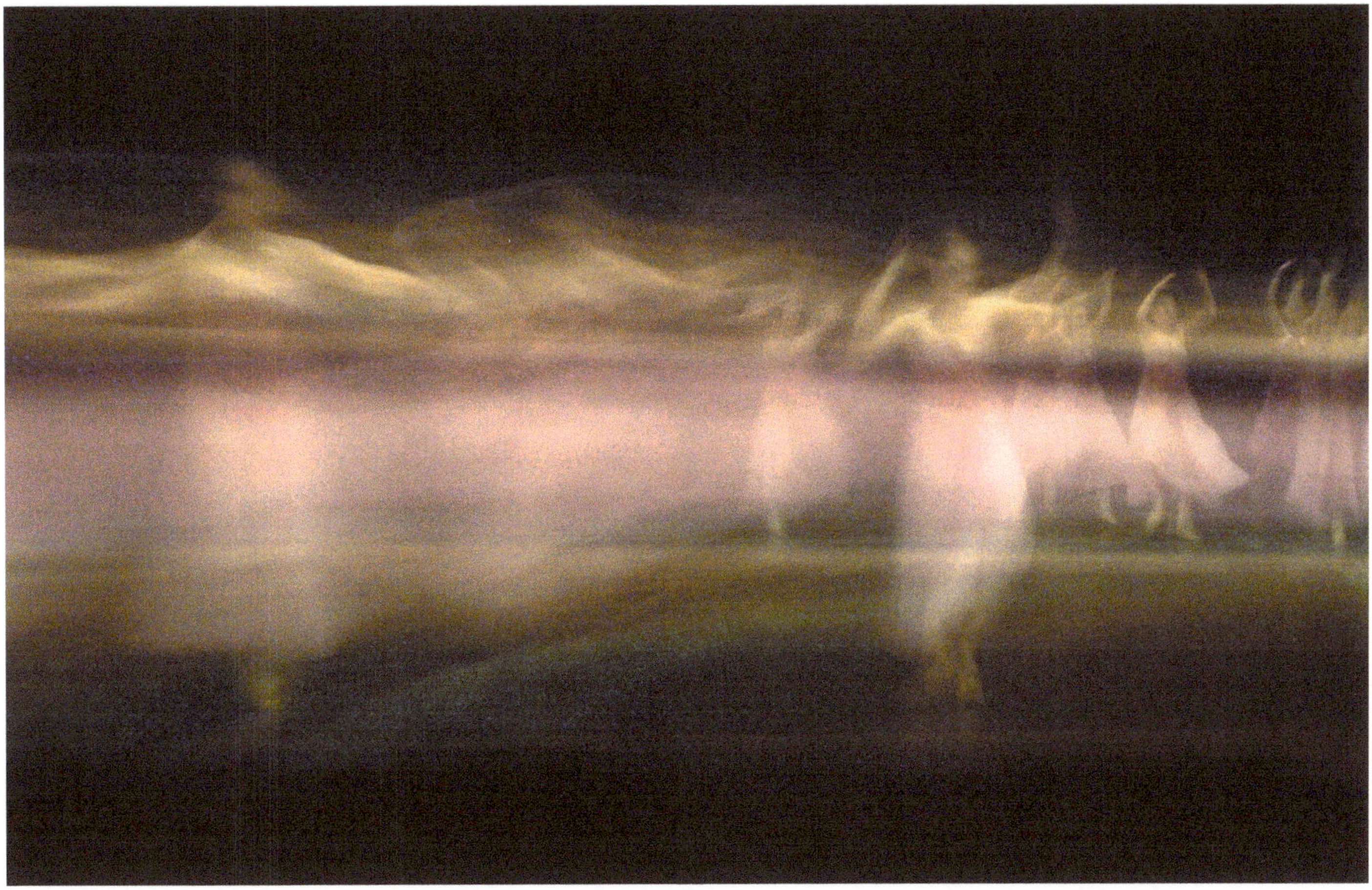

Stillness

As I begin to write,
I listen for the voice in my head
that will tell me what direction my heart needs to go.

All ideas and gifts start from a place
that can only be touched with a still and pure mind.

Know that all great things will come,
when you can operate from a place of stillness.

It is here that all ideas will take form.

Listen Deep

You know that when you ask these questions,
you will always know the answers.

Look in deep and see what is there.

Everyone has the ability to listen deep.
You have to quiet the mind for this to happen.

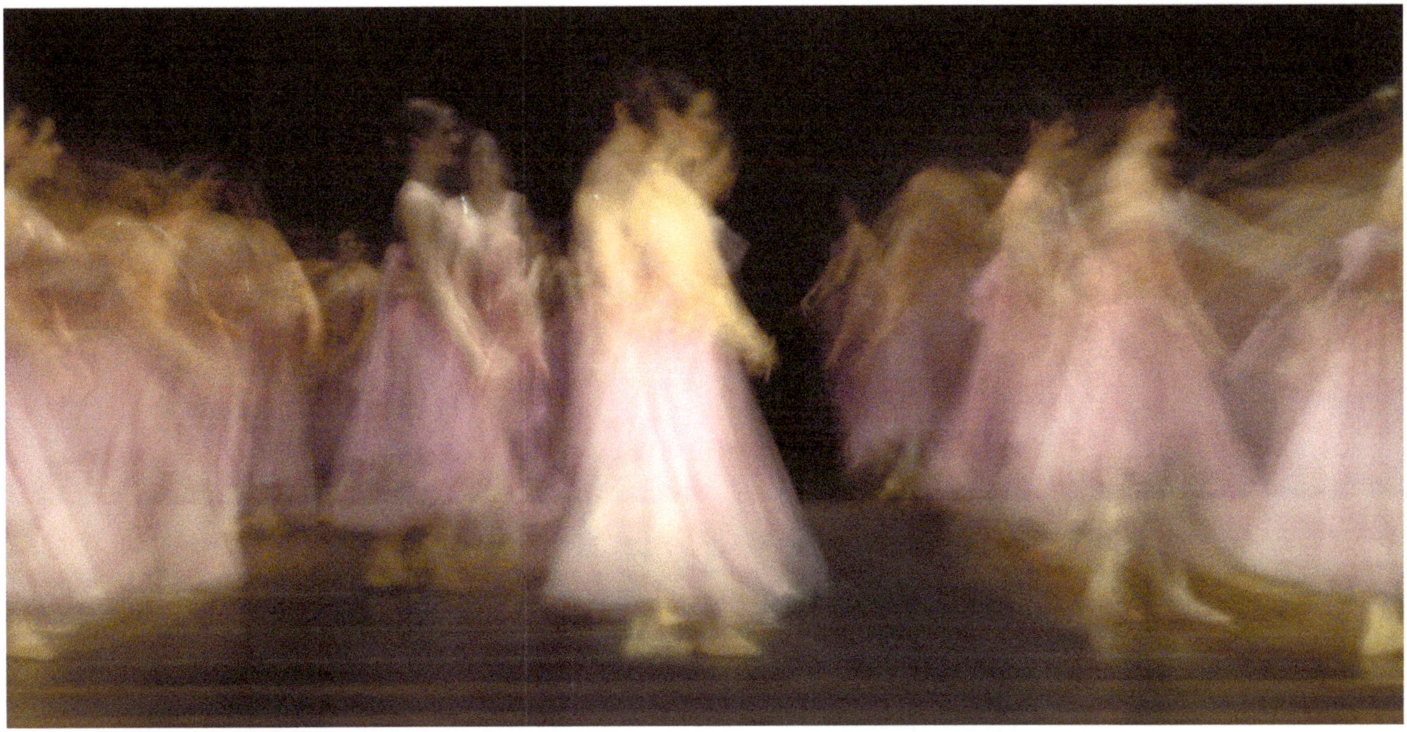

Cluttered Thoughts

Do not question what is in your head.

It is coming from a place that
can only be touched with a still mind.

The sounds of life clutter my thoughts.

You have to go in deep when this happens
and know that you have the ability to
listen to your Soul.

It is always there sending messages to you,
whenever you are available.
This can be at any moment in time…

All it takes is for you to stop and listen.

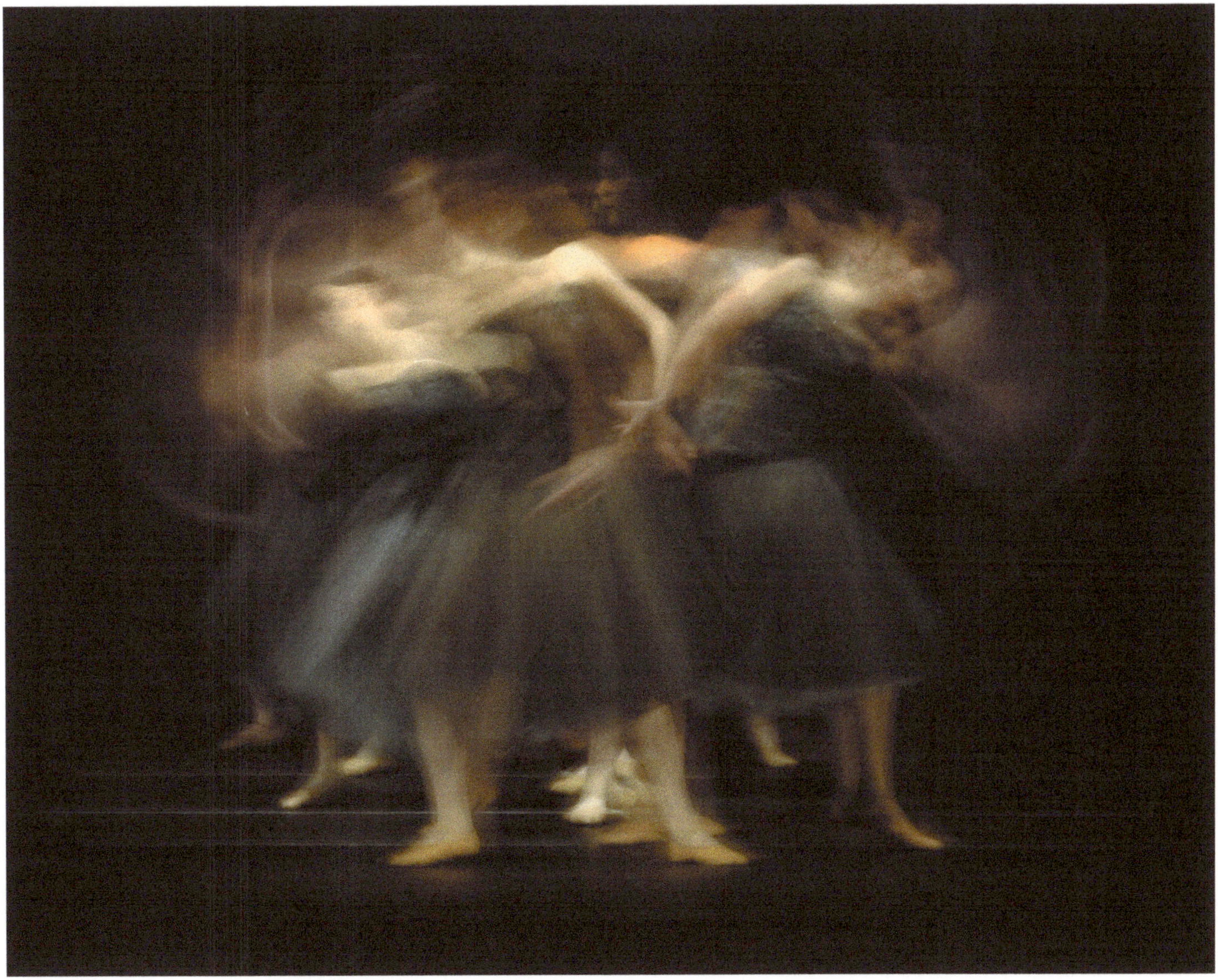

Pondering Life

As I sit pondering the meaning of life,
I have to wonder whether by sitting and pondering…

Am I actually missing life?

Listen to what your heart tells you.
If you want to sit, sit.

Being aware of what your Soul is telling you,
is the way to achieve true happiness.

Nothingness

I never push myself too hard…
If I am tired, I rest.

My body craves the stillness and quiet.
It is in this place,
that I am able to hear my true self.

It is an art to be able to just
sit and do nothing.

You will find that within this nothingness…
true art is found.

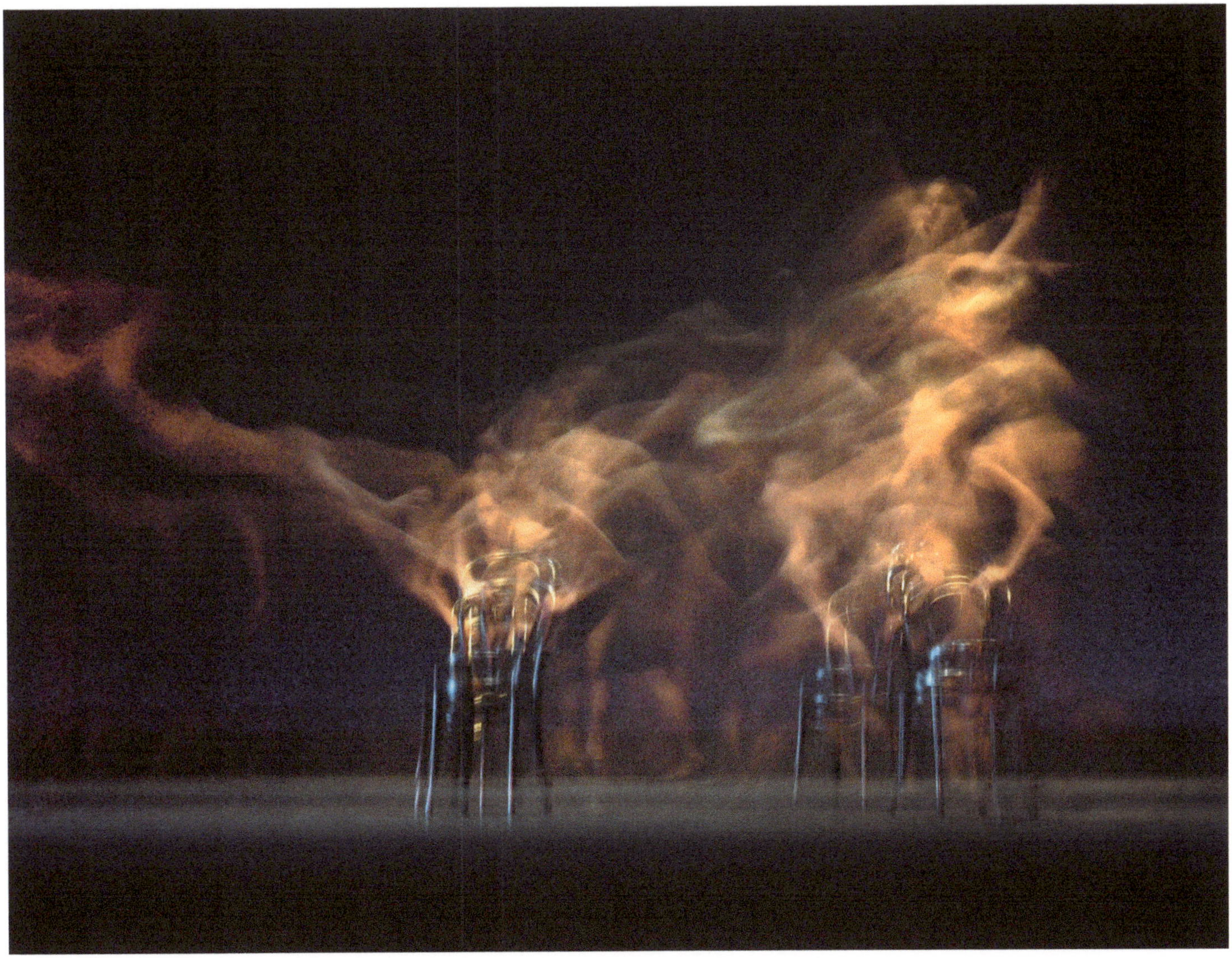

Finding Truth

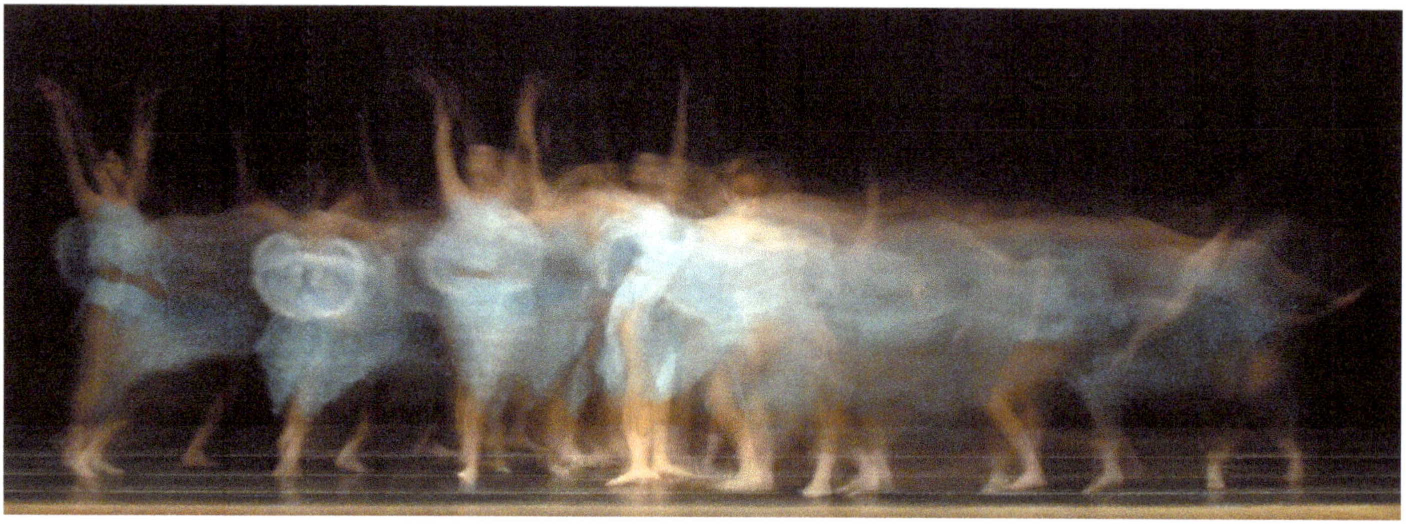

Inner Truth

I'm looking in deep, to see what comes out…
I'm anxious at the possibility of such greatness.

My light is so strong, it burns away any doubt.

You must go in. It is the only way to find your truth.

The outside is just a playground to express your dreams, which are created from within.

All is possible… Just listen.

Happiness

There is happiness in truth…
The truth is who you are right now.

If you can accept your truth…
You can be happy.

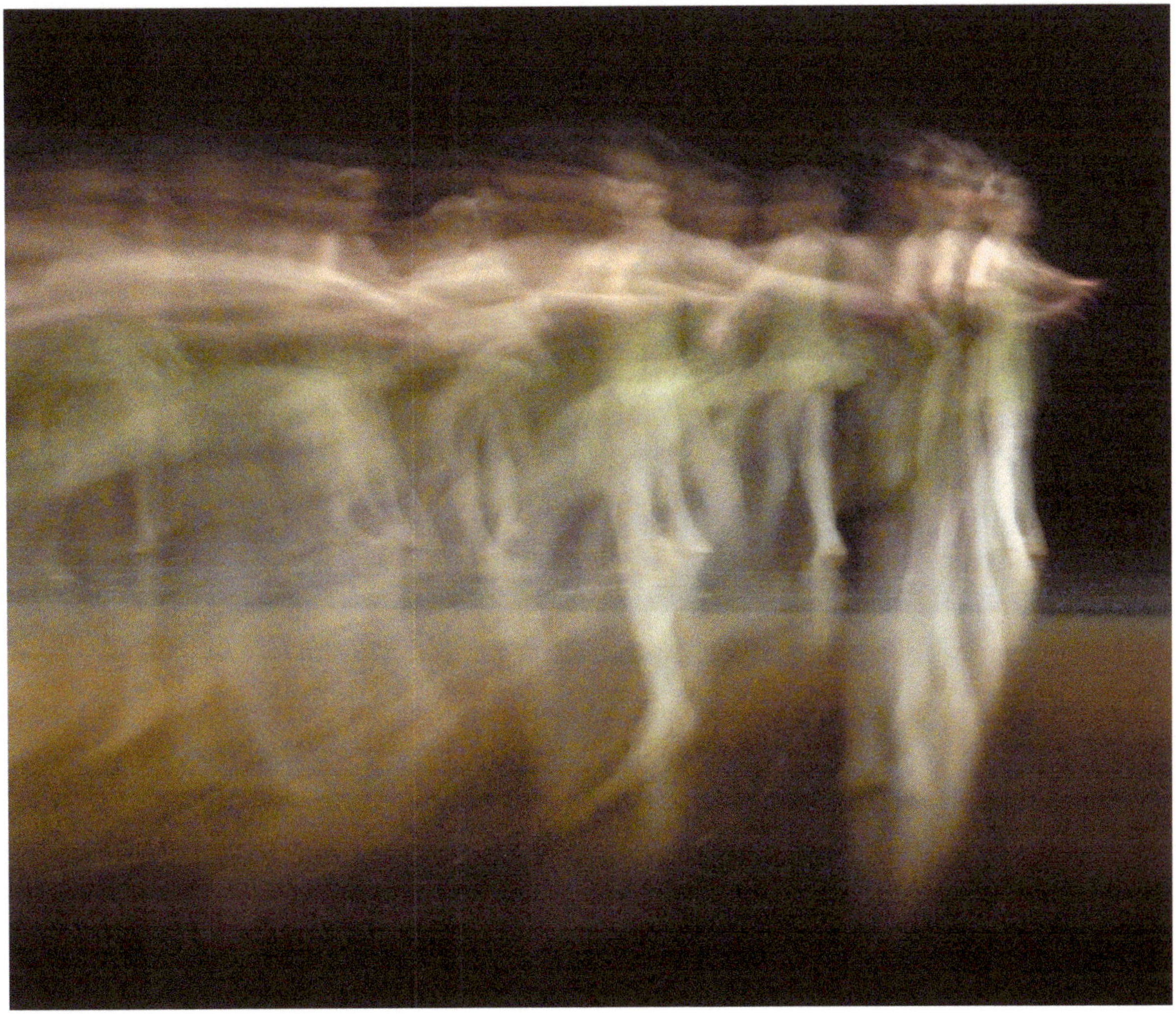

Your Thunder

The sound of the thunder reminds me,
that there is a greater voice that teaches us about life.

Listen to that voice and all truths will be uncovered.

Just as the rain pours from the clouds,
your Soul will share the many gifts that are yours.

Listen to your own thunder.

Thunder's Voice

The thunder's voice is loud and strong.

It calls me to my purpose.
It longs for me to succeed.
It guides me with certainty.
It has a knowing that if I follow my inner thunder,
I will never lose my path.

When we listen to that inner voice,
we can never lose our path...
It will always be made clear.

Just listen…
All will be shown to you, if you will just listen.

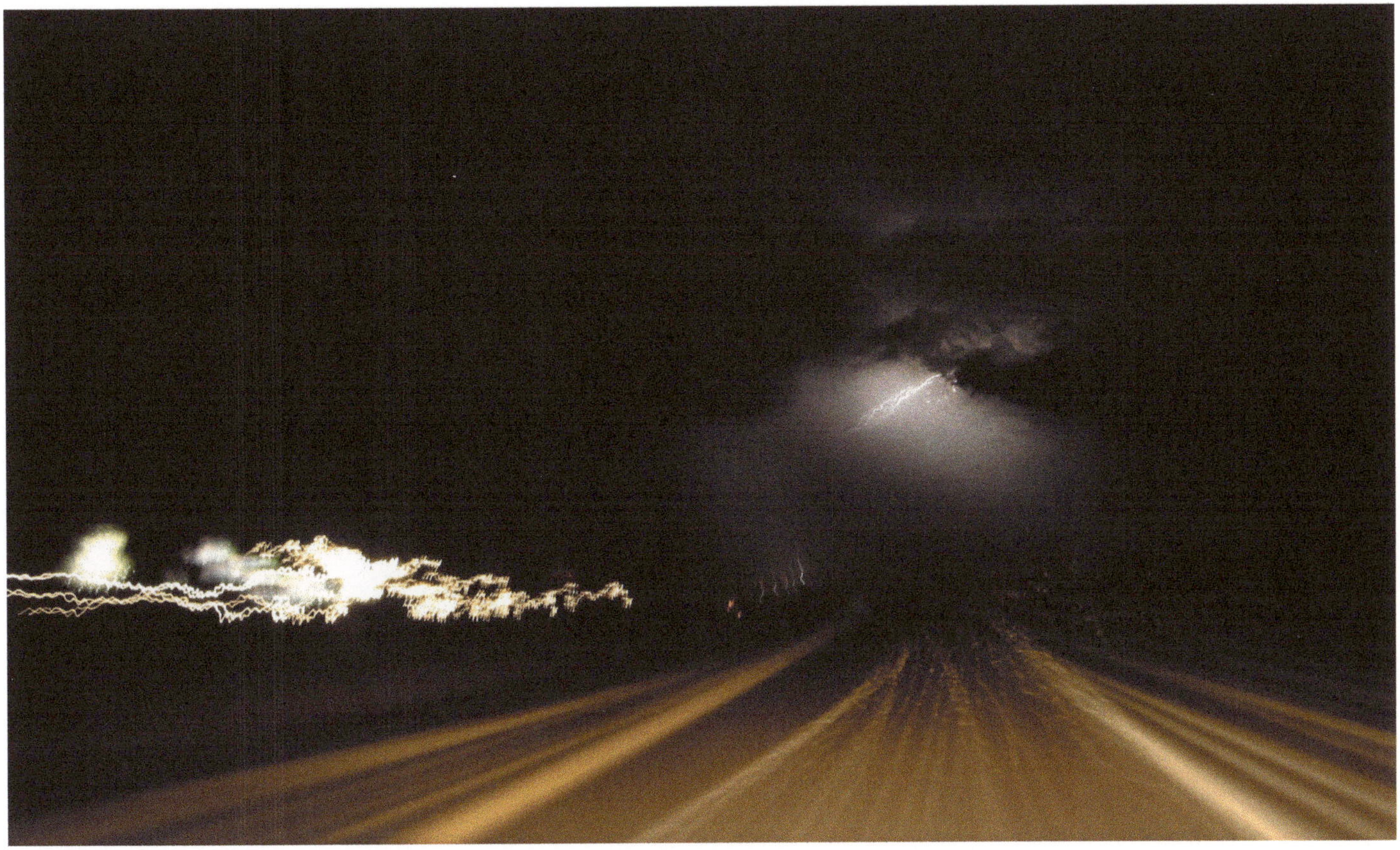

Soul Force

The mind is a powerful force.
But even more powerful, is the force of the Soul.
It will push forward in all instances when it is welcomed.

Feel great and watch the creative power at work.

When things are not forced…
all truths can come forward willingly.

We all have creative will.

Open yourself up to the power that is there…
You will always be amazed at your greatness.

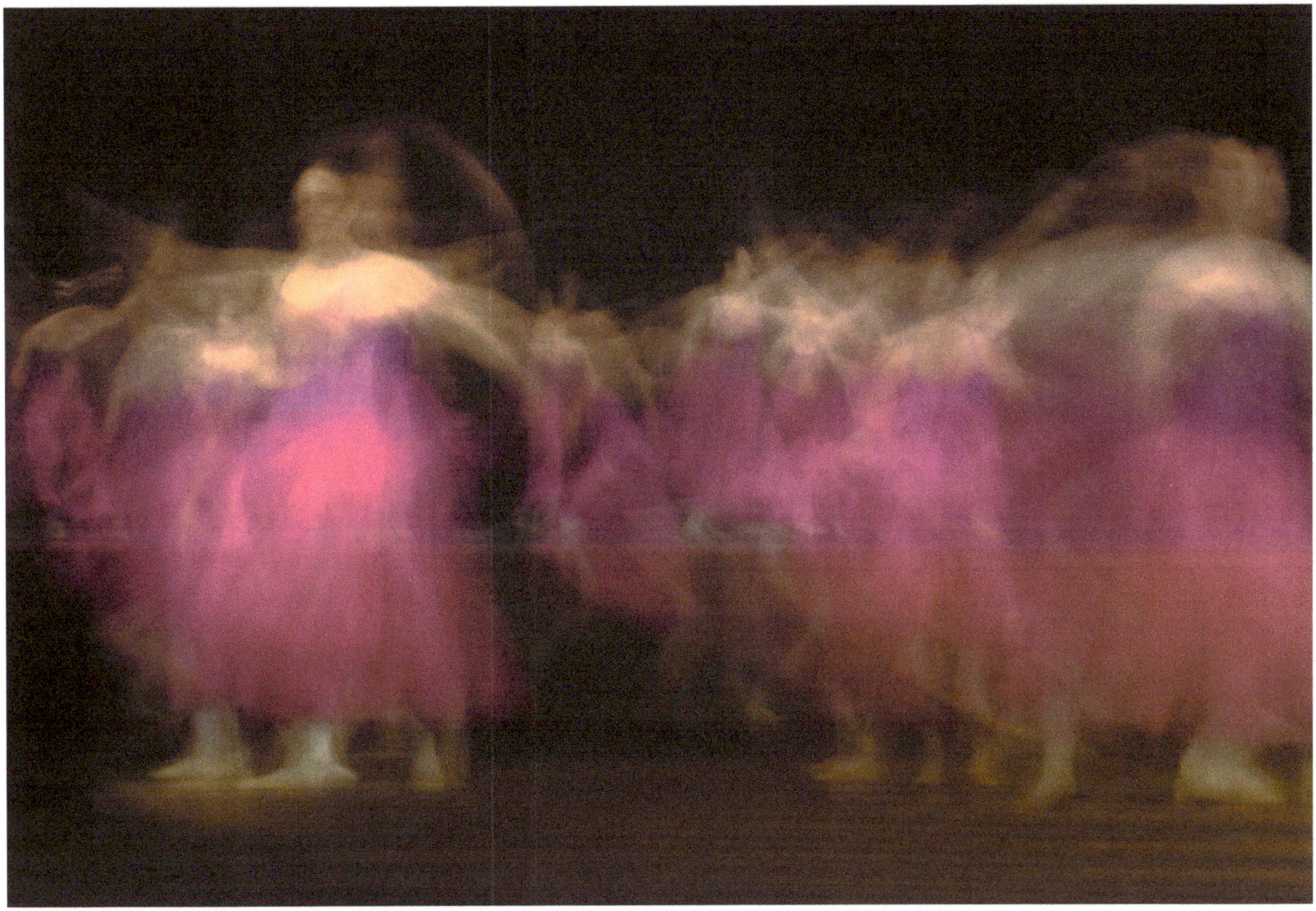

Your Truth

You can never be anything less than your
true self at any given moment in time.

It is only your perceptions that might make you
believe you have lost your truth.

From time to time, the passing clouds may
seem to hide your true self...

But know it is always there, ready to peak through
as the clouds move by... and they always do.

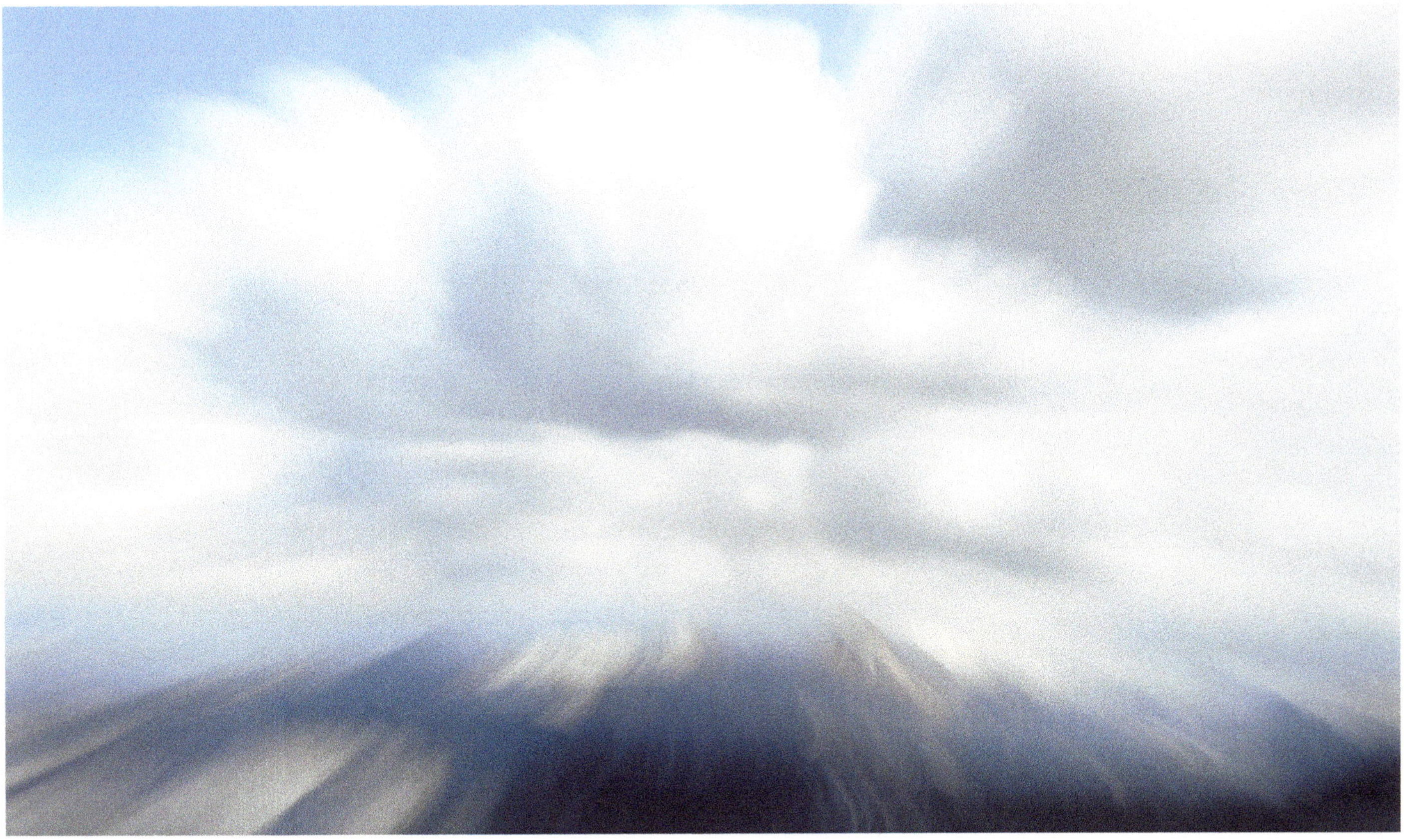

Open Soul

When the clouds open up,
the rain becomes heavy.

When we open up our Soul,
the many gifts we have will come
pouring out with great force.

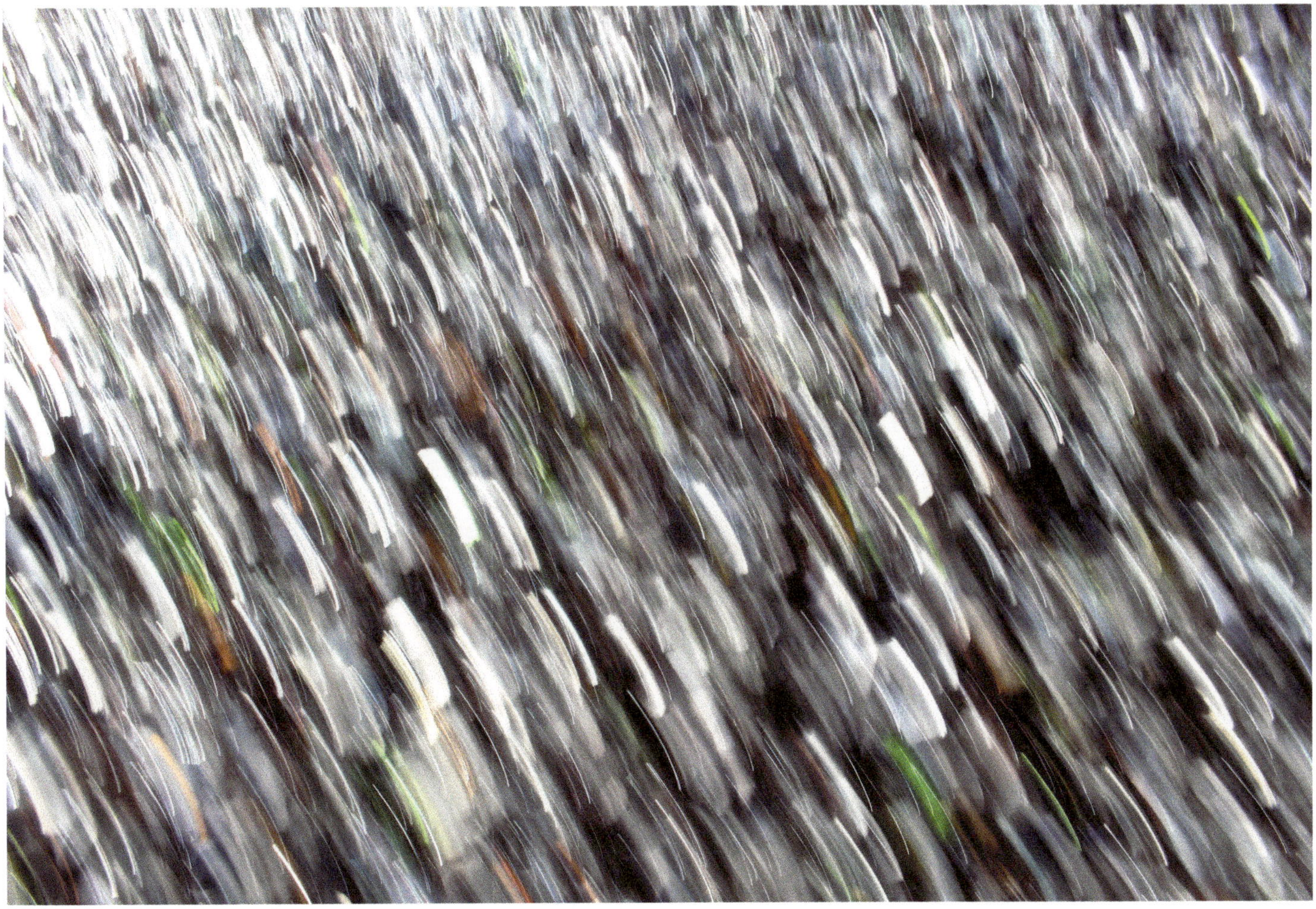

<u>Finding Truth</u>

Life is about uncovering your truths.

Year by year, layer by layer…
until your pure Soul shines through.

Once your truth has been uncovered…
it can never be hidden again.

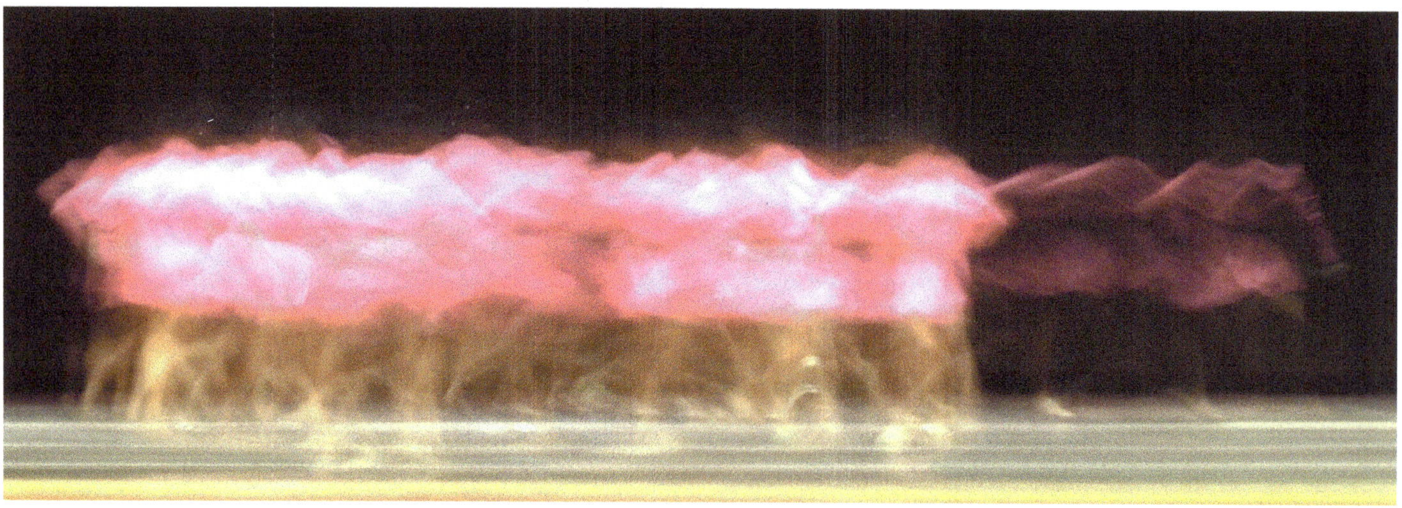

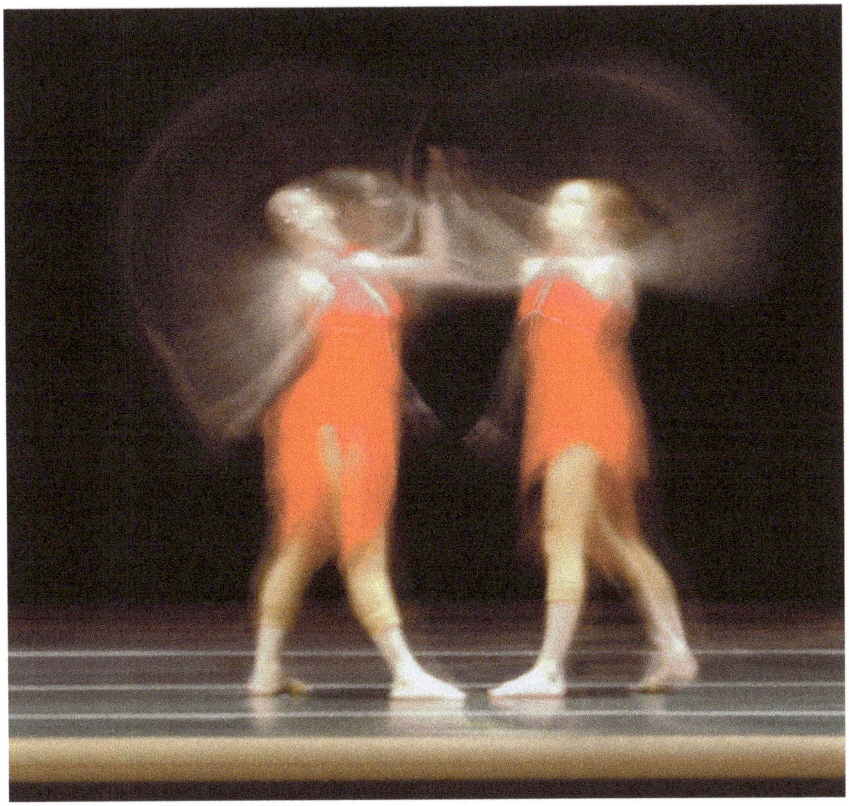

Imperfect Self

As I rub the rough edge of my Birthday Heart Rock...
It reminds me that there is always perfection in imperfection.

There is strength in being fragile.
There is beauty in being unique.
There is wisdom in age.

We need to embrace our imperfect self...
It is from within this state that great perfection is achieved.

Letting Go

When there is a constant pull from your mind
to hold onto what you think is truth.

You must realize,
when you hold onto something...
it cannot be free.

When something is held captive....
it cannot survive.

It is only by letting go,
that you will free your truths, so they can become reality.

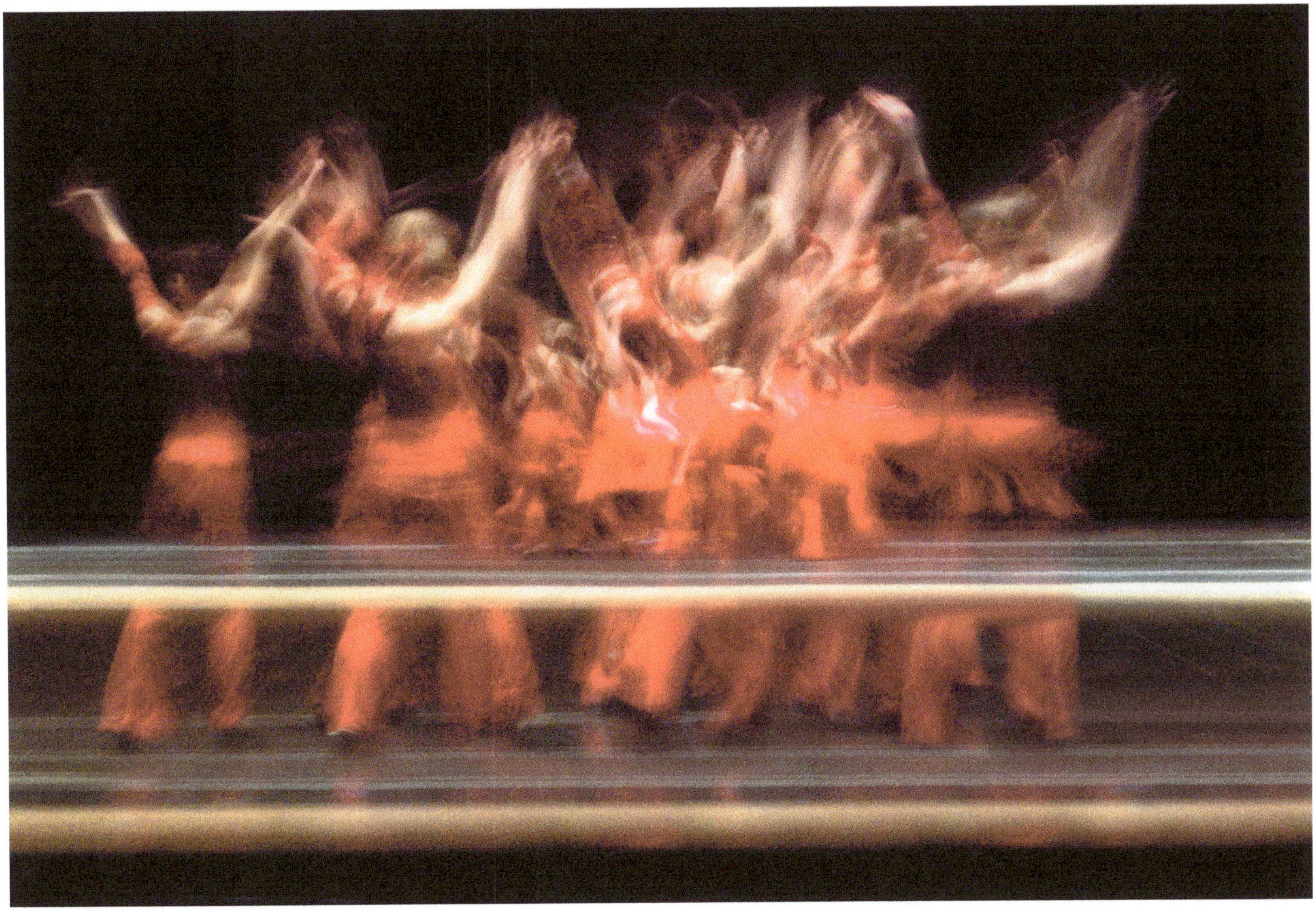

Creativity and Inspiration

Creativity

Every mind has the ability to let the Soul be creative.

We are all artists of our own destiny.

Whether you create with love or fear…
the art you make will determine your path.

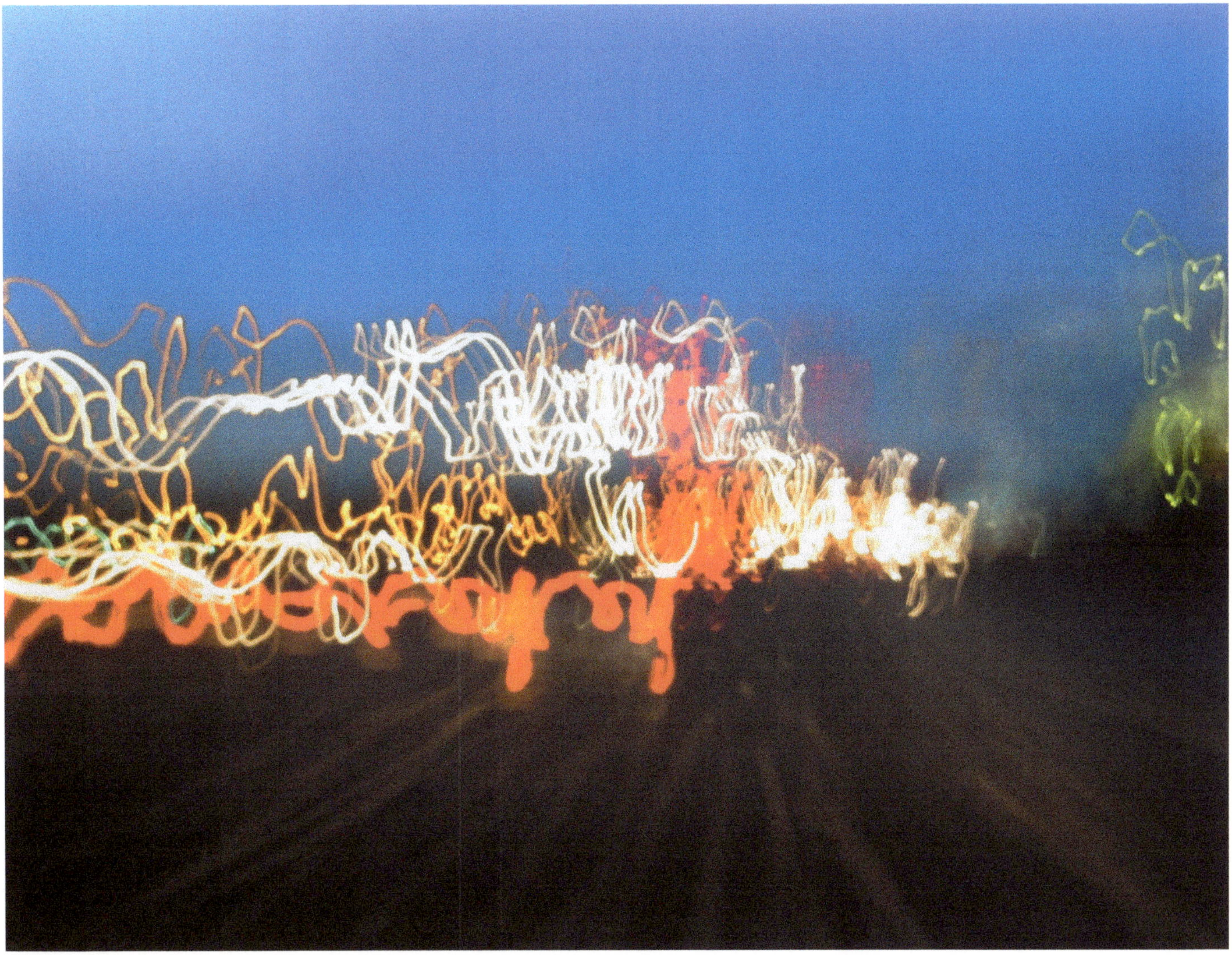

Inspiration

There is inspiration everywhere you look.
You can find life in all things.

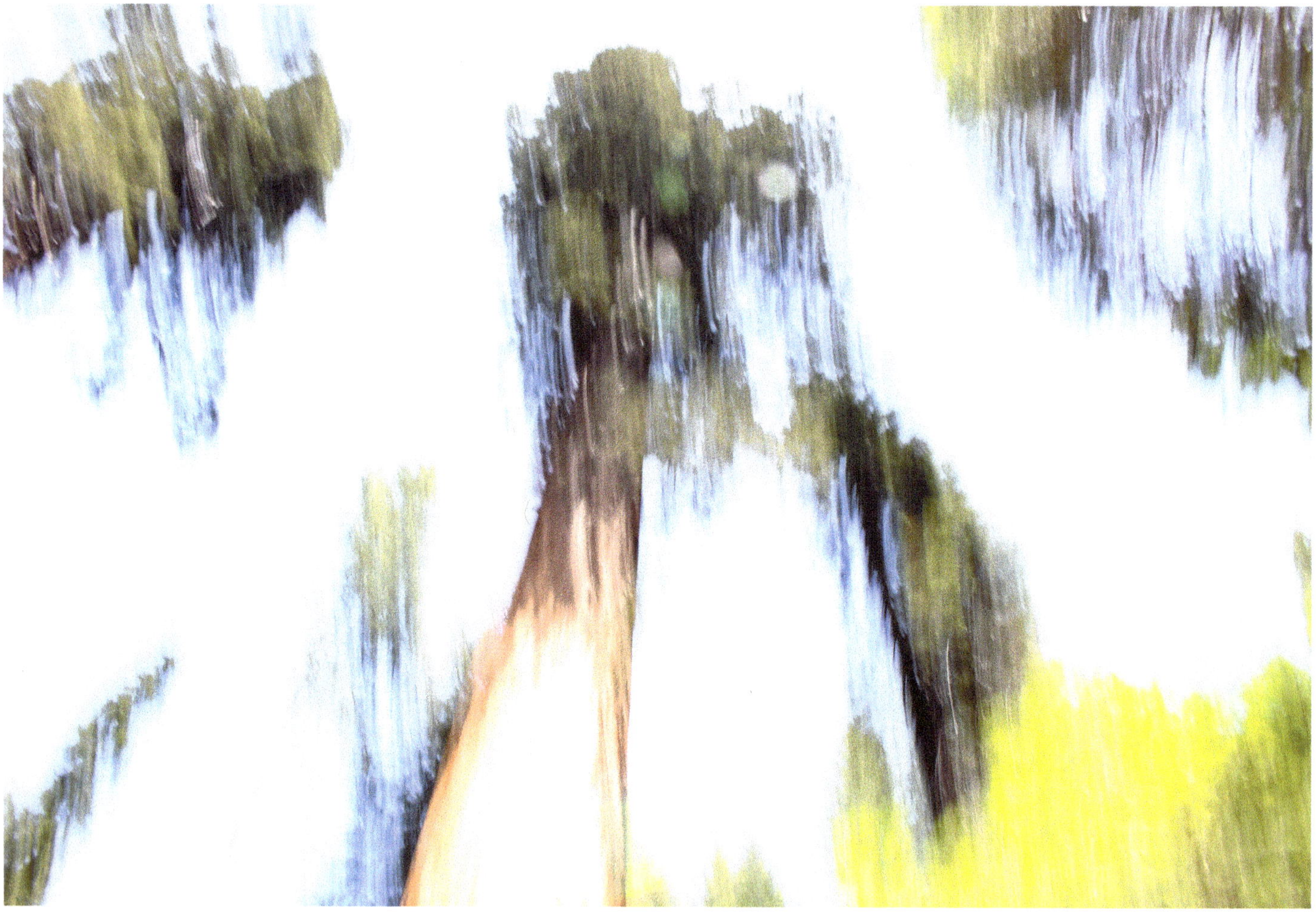

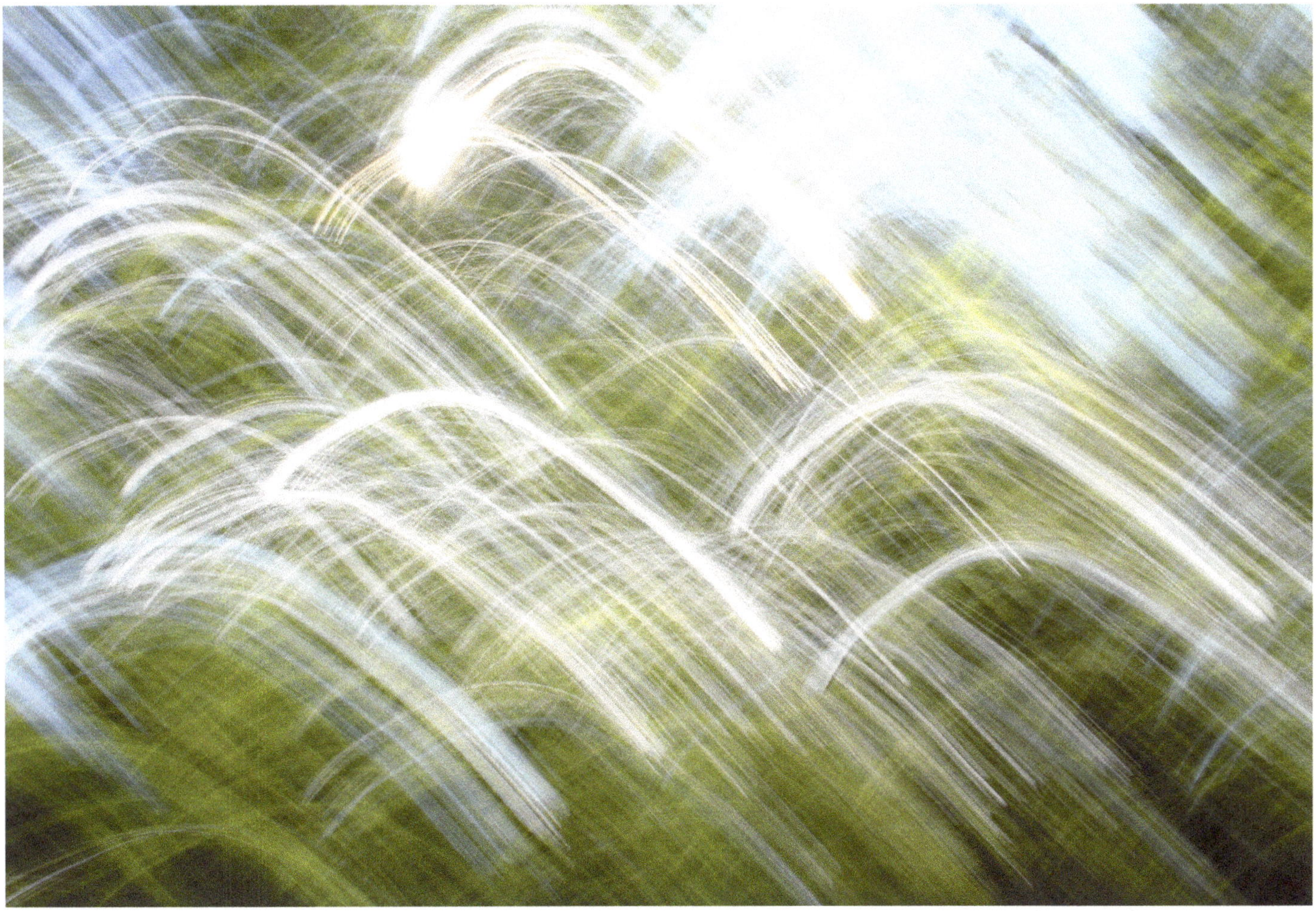

Soul Painting

When you paint from your Soul...
all humanity will understand your message.

Heart Rock Beach

My Soul is happy as I sit amidst the rock and sand.

The sound of the waves gives me an
energy I did not know I had.

The cool feel of the rocks beneath me,
radiate a calming feeling.
It draws me to them... I could stay here forever.

Heart rocks surround me everywhere I look.
Tears fill my eyes at the beauty... I feel home.
I want time to stand still, so I can be here forever.

The sun moves in and out as the tide mimics the motion.
The reflection of the wet sand holds the image of the sky.

Click, click, click...
Inspiration is overtaking me.
This beach calls me.

I must go back, but I cannot bring myself to move.
I feel grounded and safe.
Everything is in balance.

I must go... sadly.

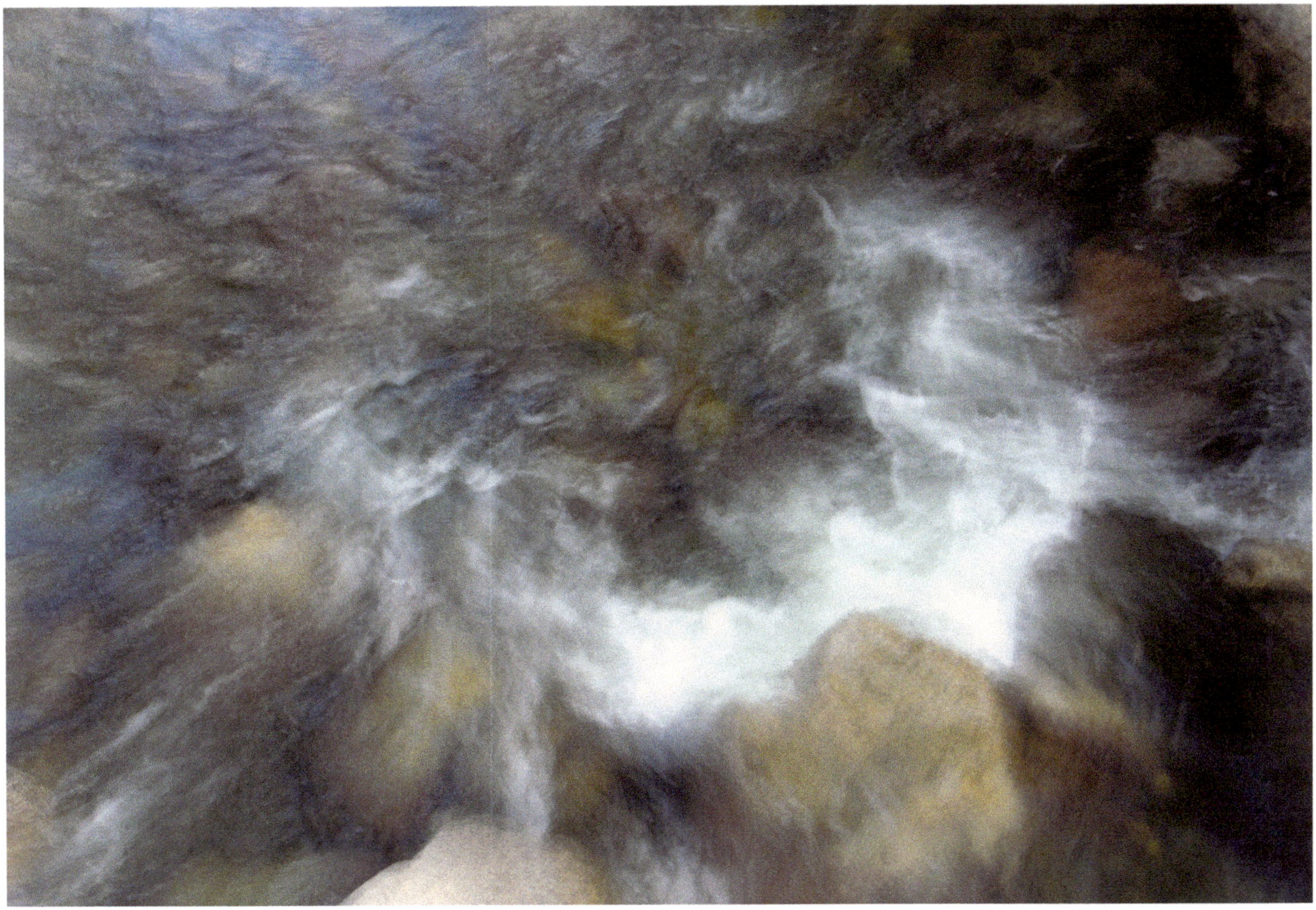

Morning Sun

Creativity stirs while the world is silent.

The morning sun brings an inspiration I did not see before.
Its light creates new possibilities.

The world awakens.

Dream

To dream is to let your Soul be free…
We all have that freedom.

Gifts

Gifts are unique.

We all have the ability to create
what is our birthright.

Listen for signs.

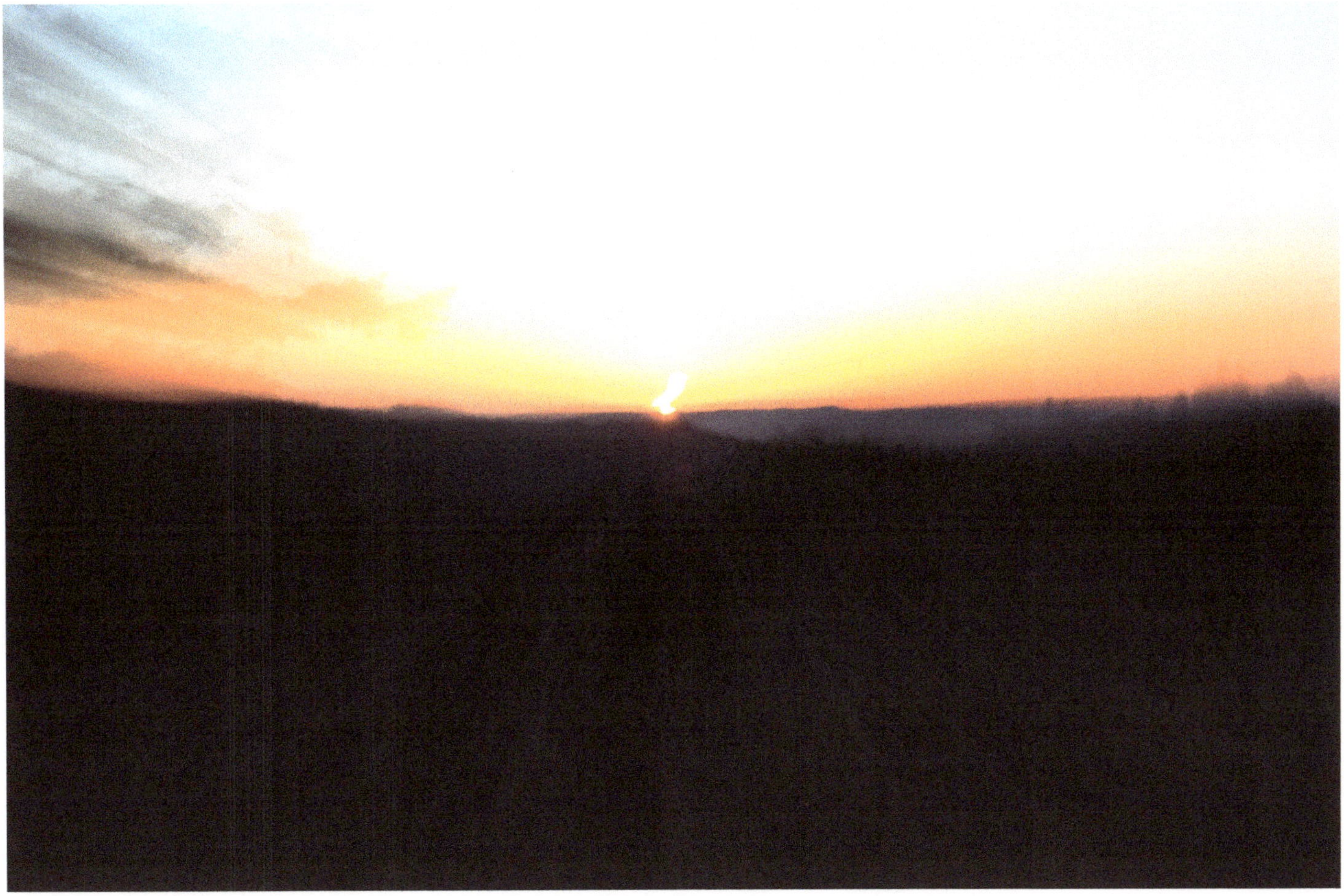

Creative Block

Creative block only comes when
you force things.

Let go...
Still the mind.

Creative Power

The day is coming to an end...
I feel peace at my accomplishments.

*Just know that to accomplish something
is to be using your creative power.*

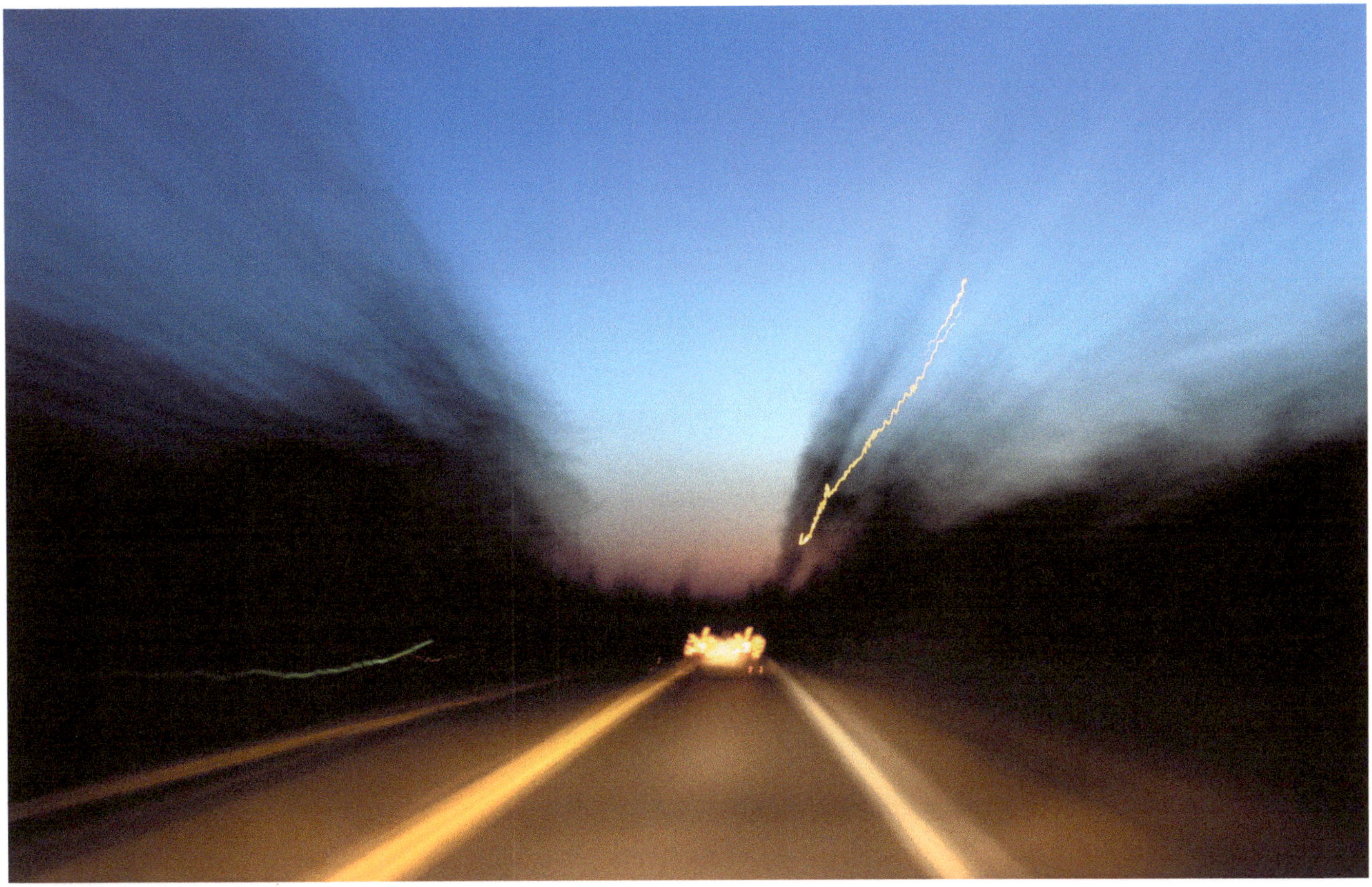

Nature

Nature

Life has many meanings.
All can be found through nature.

When you hear a bird sing;
when you see a hawk fly.

Take notice.

Look at a flower; smell the scent.
Feel the breeze on your cheek.

Notice how you feel… It is all there.

Live in the present moment and you will
experience the most that life has to offer.

This is everyone's gift.
Take it, it is yours.

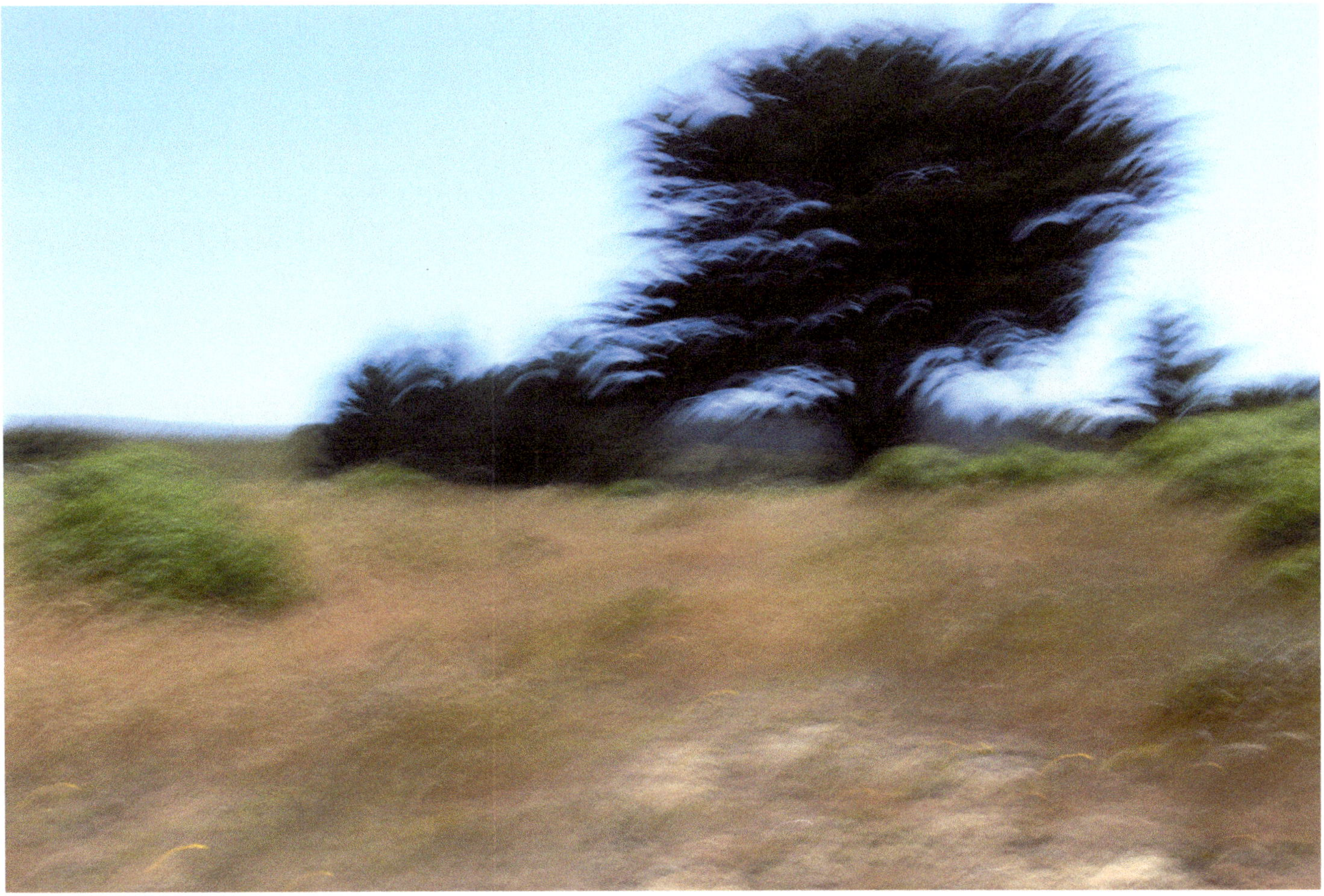

Nature Language

The birds mimic the sound in my head.
What messages do they bring?

Learn the language of nature
and you will have a deep understanding
of what life is.

Morning Song

The birds wake up singing...
happy to be alive.

Even before the light of day shines through,
they know it is coming.

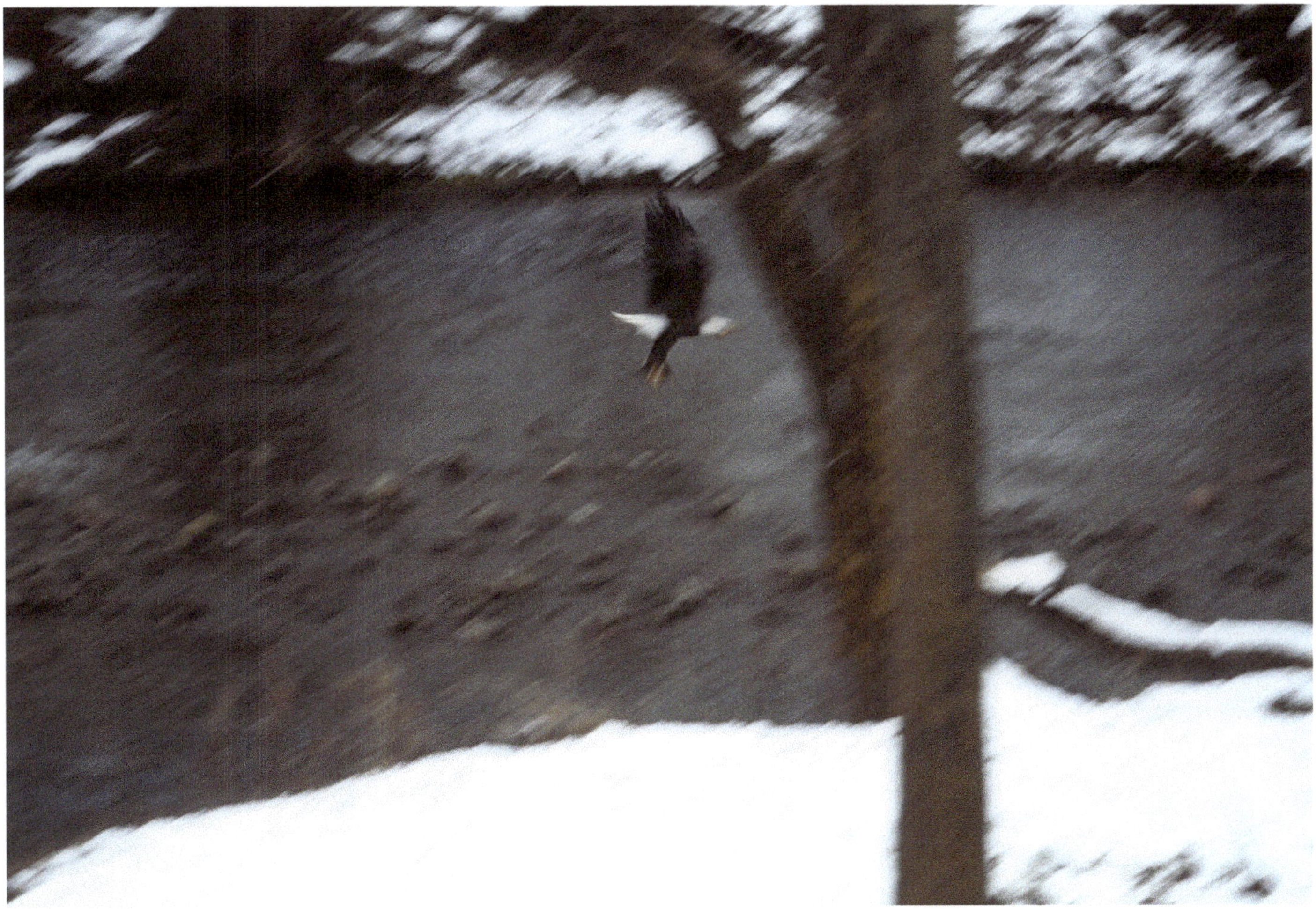

<u>Nature's Orchestra</u>

As I sit listening to the sounds of
thunder in the distance,
I wonder at nature's orchestra.

The creek flows…

Rain sounds…

Just meditate to the sounds of nature,
it will soothe your Soul like no other method.

It is music from heaven…
perfectly orchestrated.

There is no sound that can
compete with nature.

Use it for all that you can.

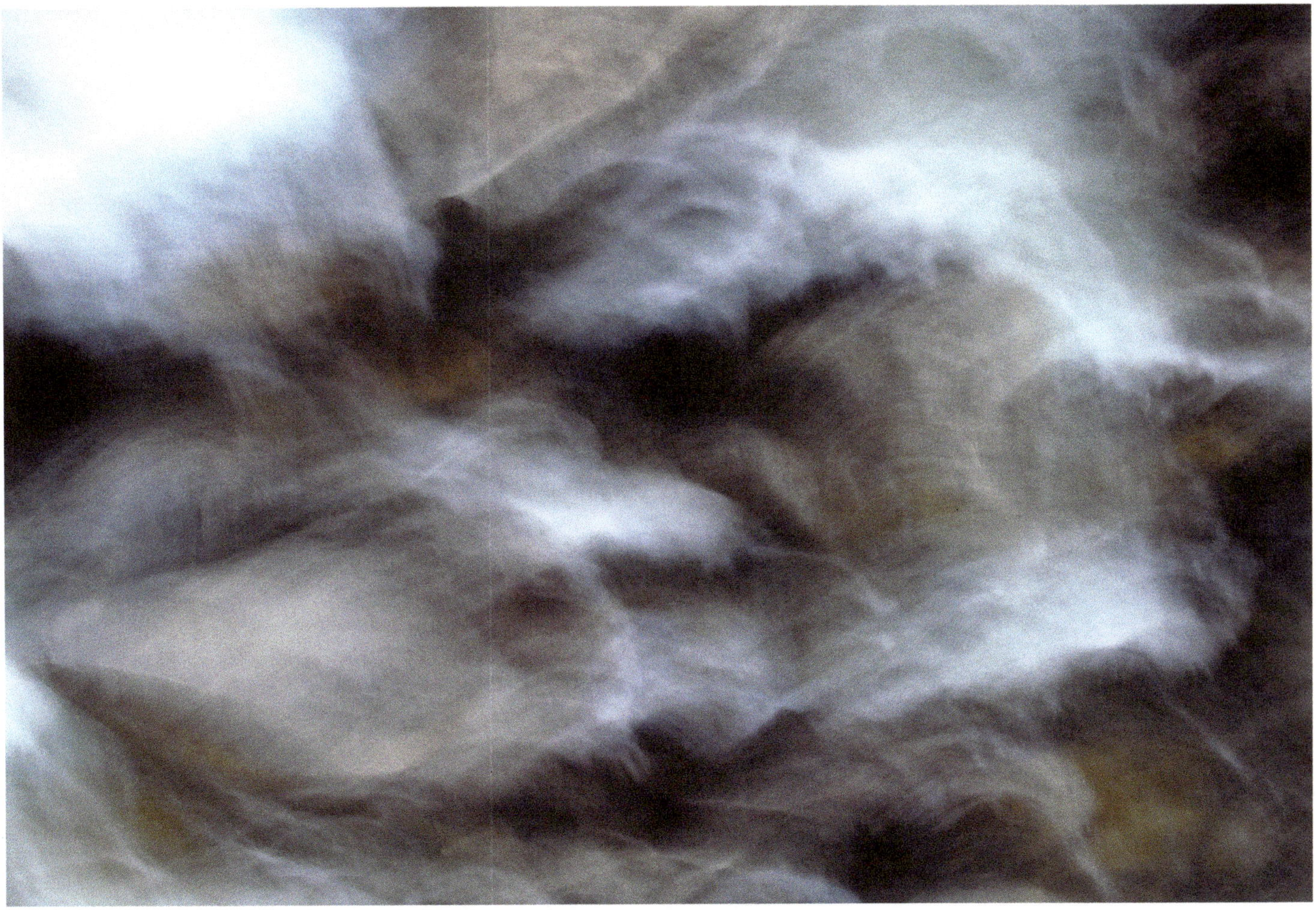

Spring is Here

The wind whistles as it touches my ear.
I feel a sense of peace.

The grass grows as spring moves on;
I sit amongst fallen branches.

My hand moves as my
Soul pushes forth a message.

Spring is here…
Time to reflect on all that is.

Move forward knowing that you have
everything you need.

All is well.

Nature's Inspiration

I feel the most creative when
I am out in nature.

Nature is the truest form of inspiration.

You will always find what you
need to create greatness.

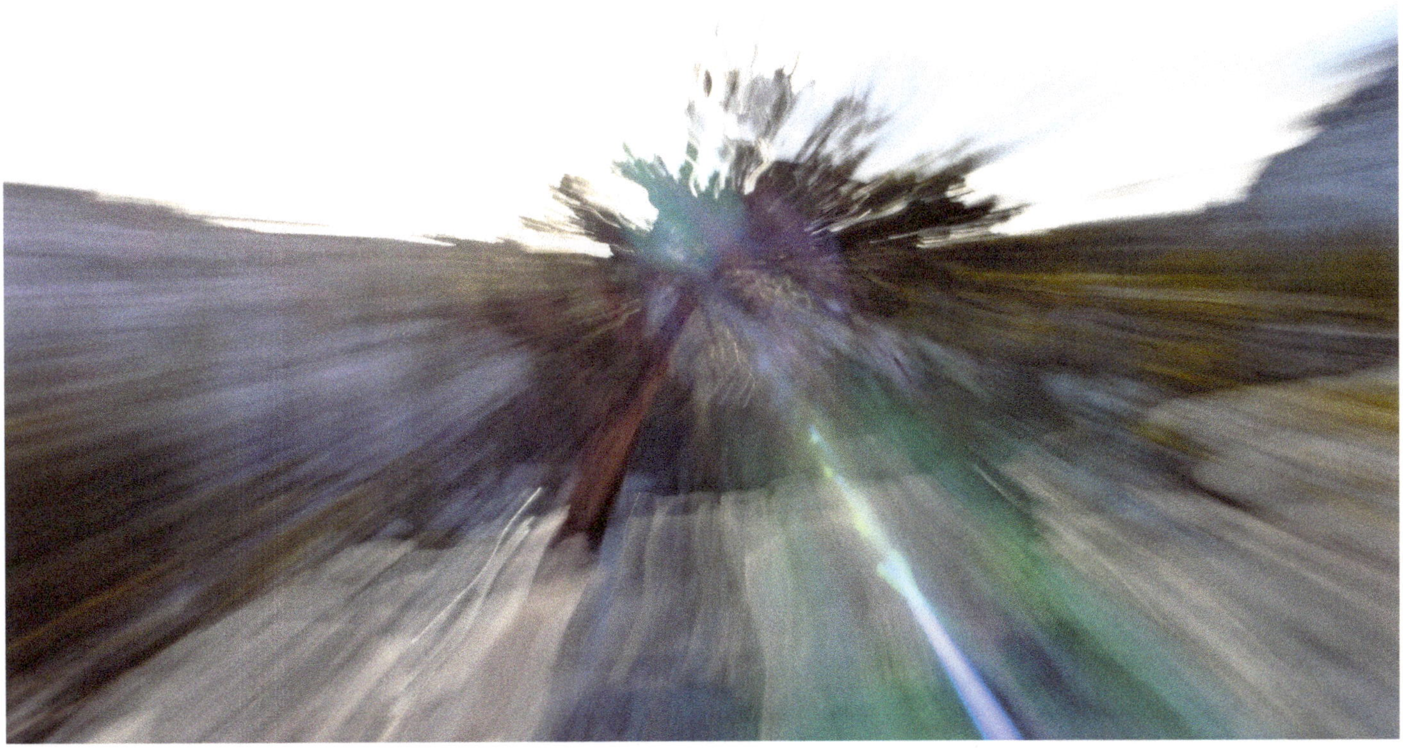

Hear the Soul

Hear the Soul

The warmth of the sun radiates
an energy…
It fills my Spirit with spring.

Life is always spring.

Be present.

Hear the Soul…
It will come through always for you.

Learn to listen to God's whisper.

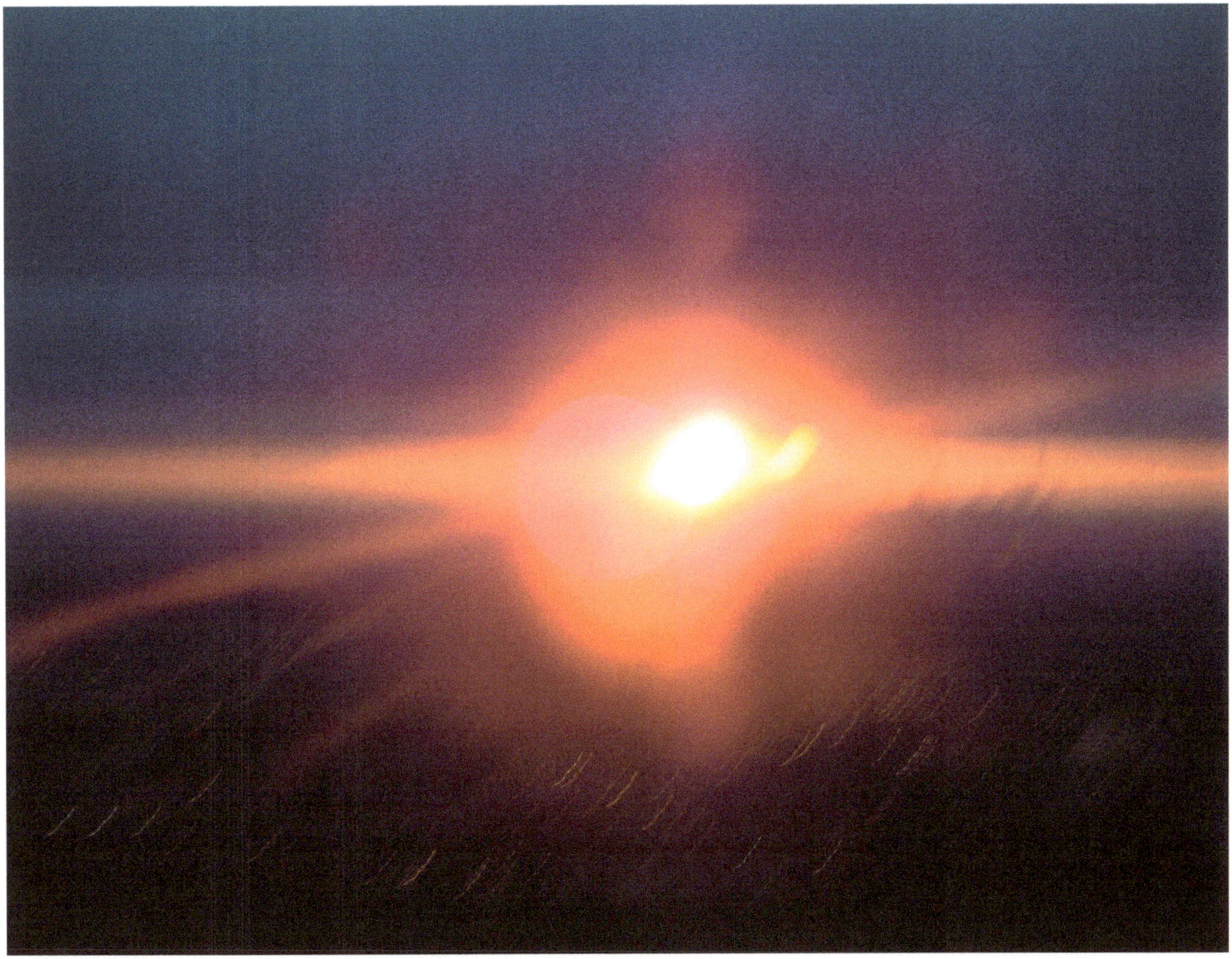

Learning Spirit

As I search to learn about Spirit...

I realize, it is only a search to confirm
what I already know.

Soul Speak

You must stop everything
when your Soul speaks...

It is a gift that cannot be put off until later.

Metaphors

You will find many messages
hidden in metaphors...

All the answers are there.

Become connected to Spirit
and everything will become clear.

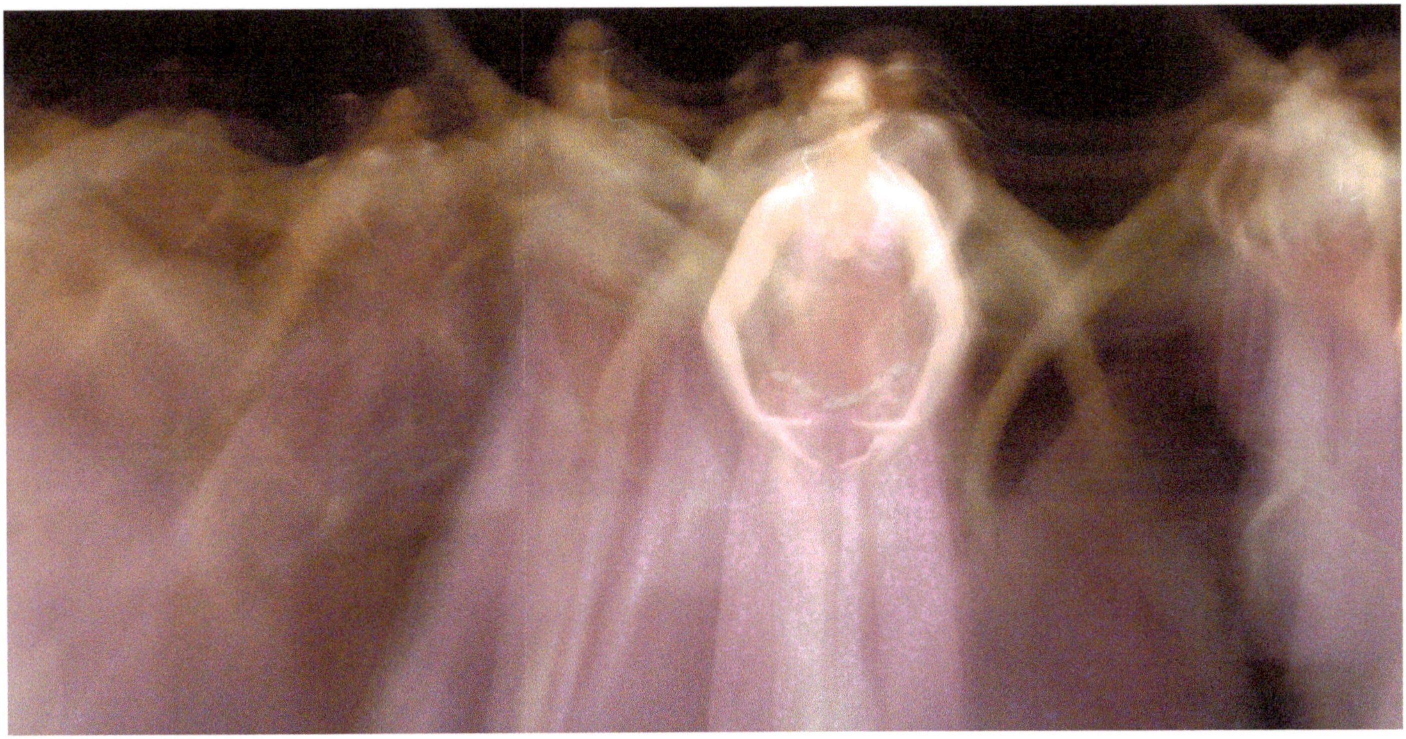

Listen

To hear is to know.
To listen is to understand.

You can't always decipher
what comes through, at the time it comes through.

Hear the world around you...

Seek out the messages that are there for you.

Confused Thoughts

Don't be confused in the thoughts you hear.

Trust that all messages have meaning.

Messages

My body is not used to rising so early.

Why is it that the best thoughts are
hidden within these quiet hours?

It is then that you can hear us better...
We have so many messages to give.

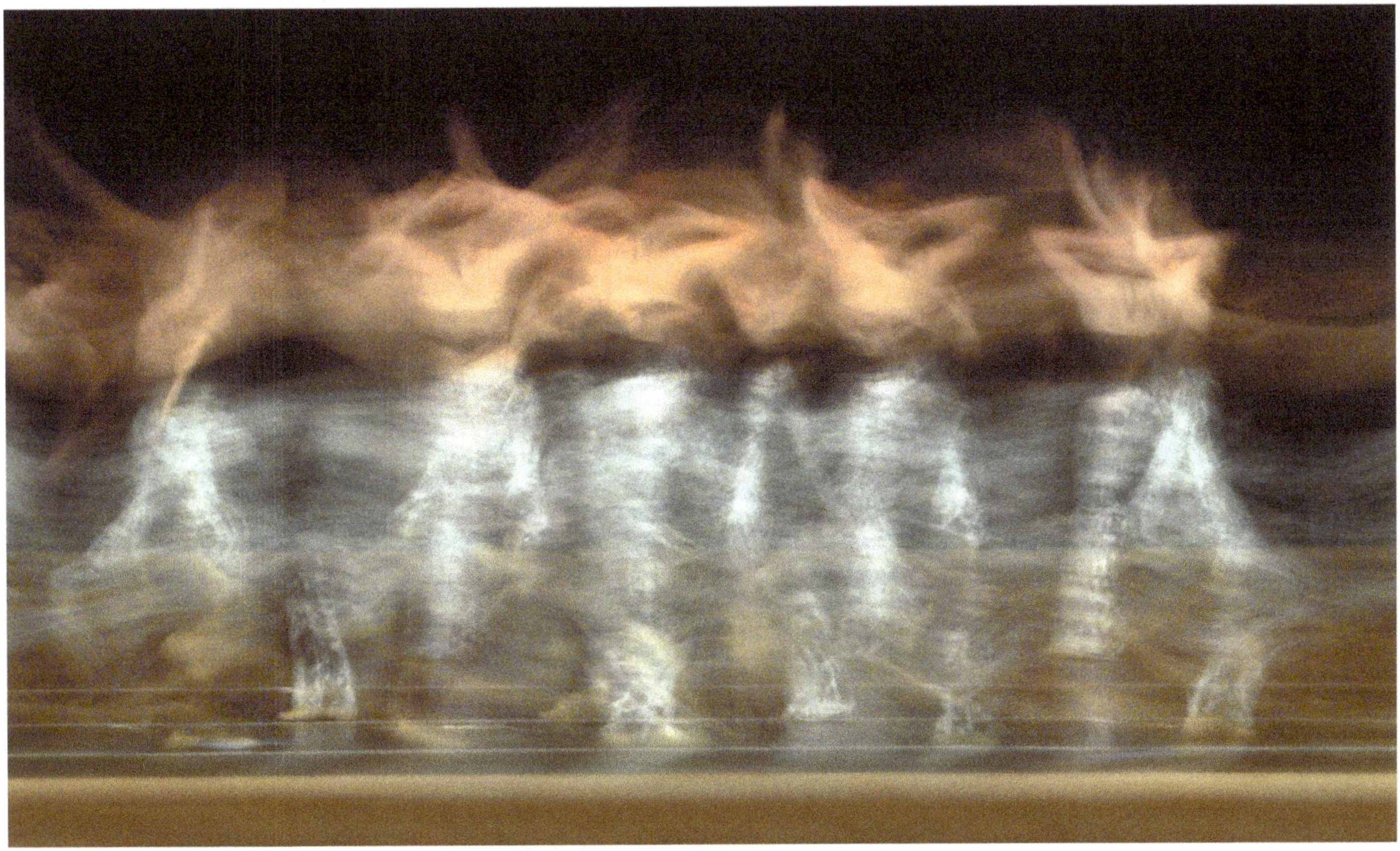

<u>Helpers</u>

I sit here wondering if what I am hearing is for real.

Abraham is the name that comes into my head.

All great ones have what we call a helper…
to help them achieve the greatness that is theirs.
You have us.

Please know to keep going,
whether or not you know what you are doing.

It will all come to you, at the time you need it to.

Never doubt in what we have in store for you.

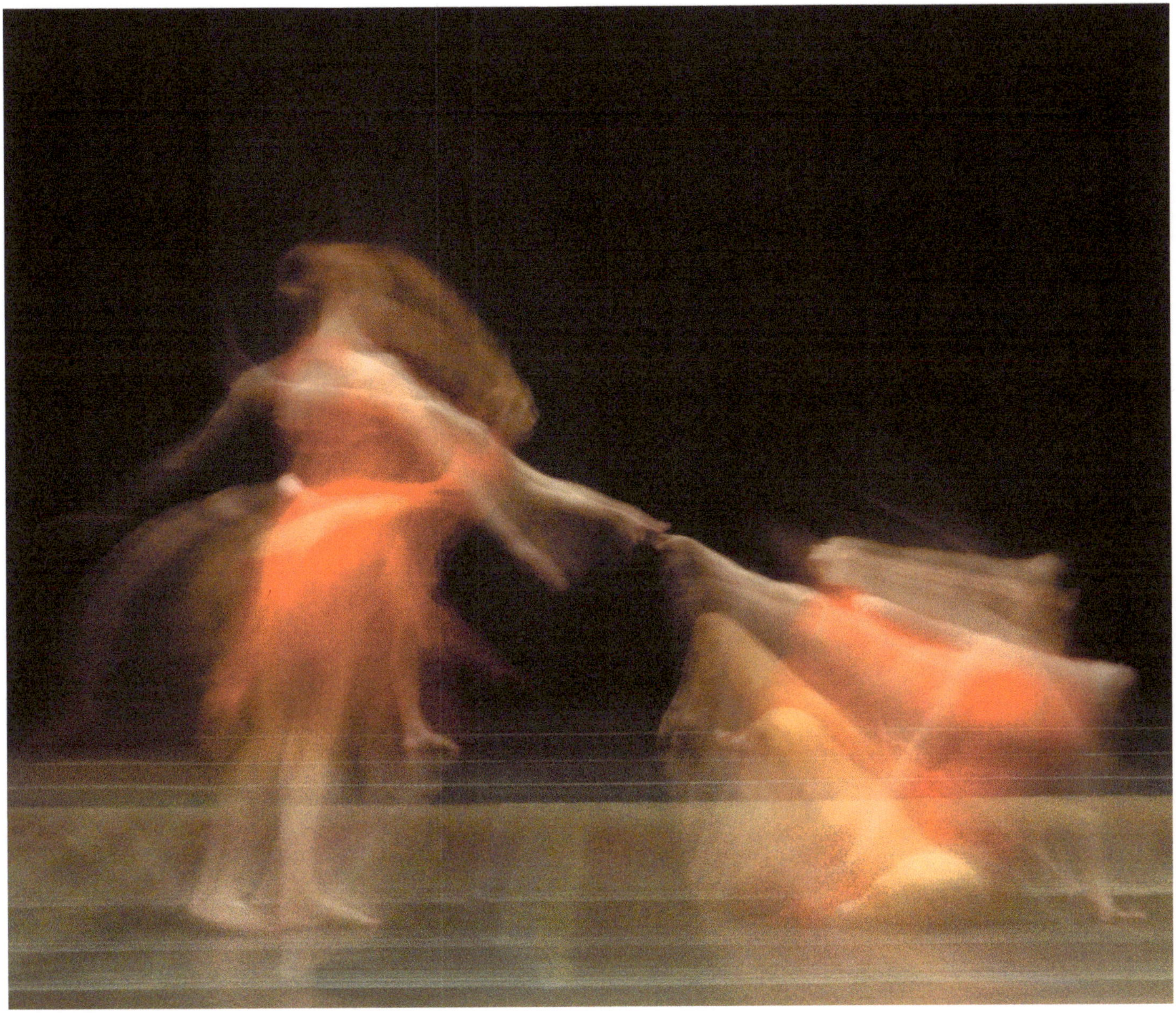

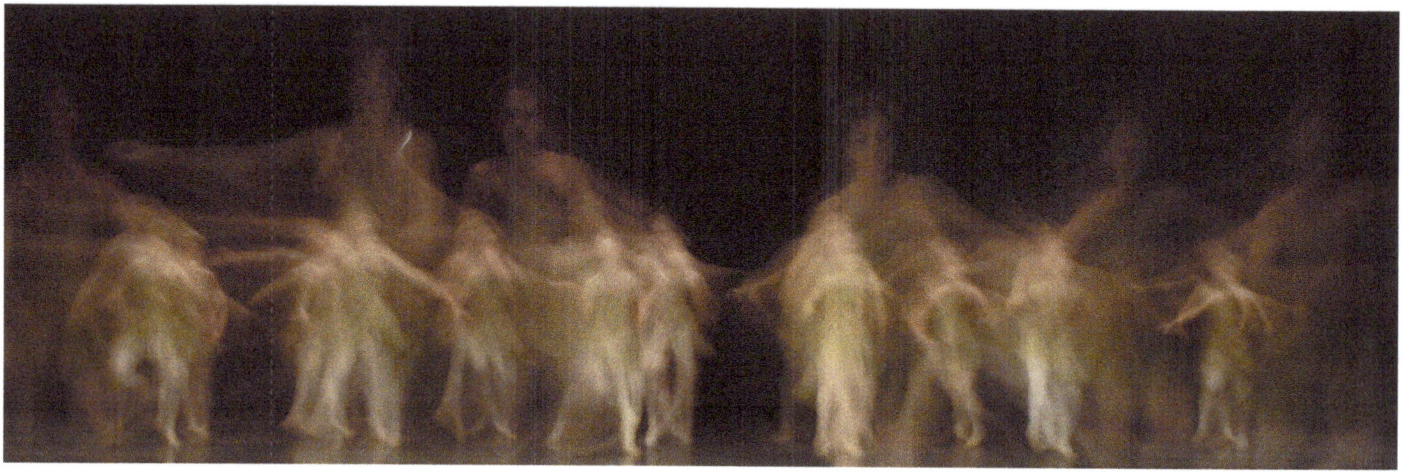

Blessings

To be given a gift is a blessing.
To be able to hear what we say is a blessing.
Please use this blessing wisely.

You will be shown everything you need to know,
when you need to know it.

Please take time to hear us.

This gift is yours to share with the world…
the meanings that you have discovered.

That is your blessing.

Where you Need to Be

Thank you for putting me where I need to be.

You are always right where you need to be…
Never doubt that.

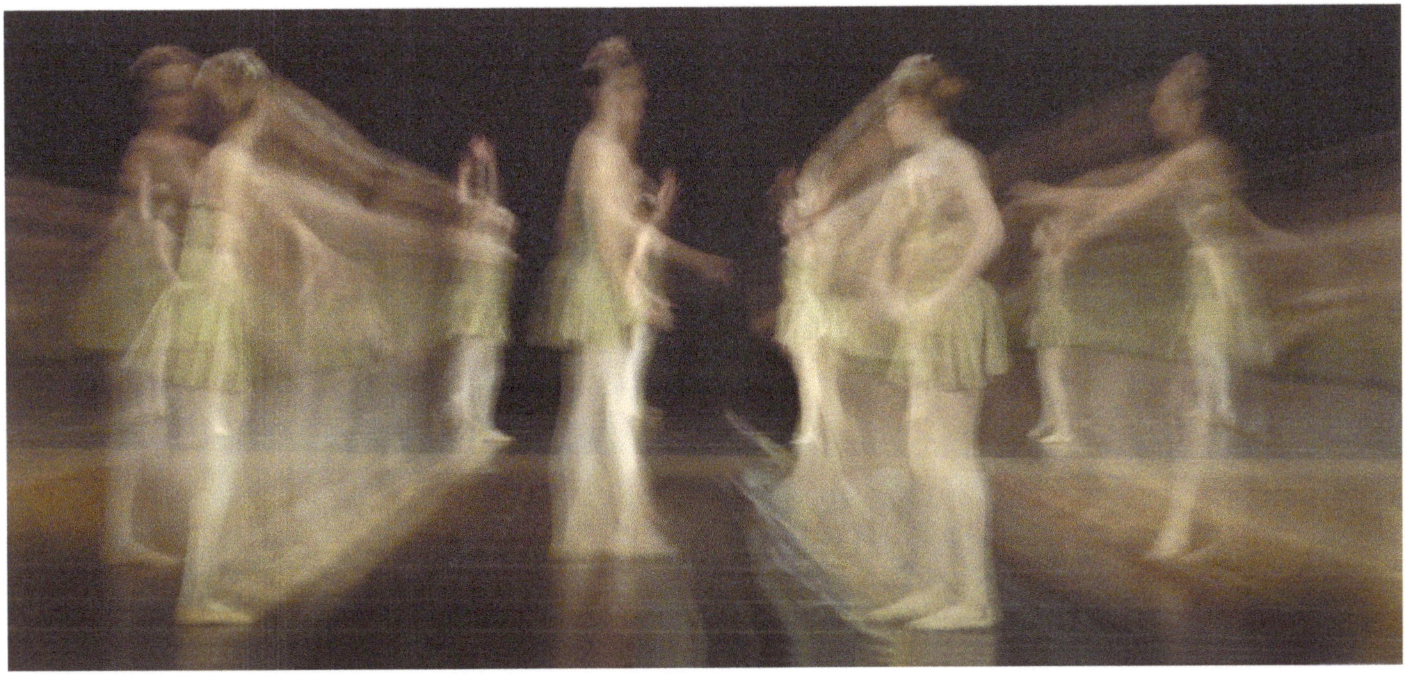

Hear our Voice

Just write.

Messages will always be heard if you will just put the pen to the paper.

I'm excited at the possibilities that are coming through me from a place that I don't yet understand.

Hear our voice…
It is the only sure thing that you have always.

Move forward with a clear mind.
If you need to take care of life, do it.

Come to us with a clear mind ready to work.

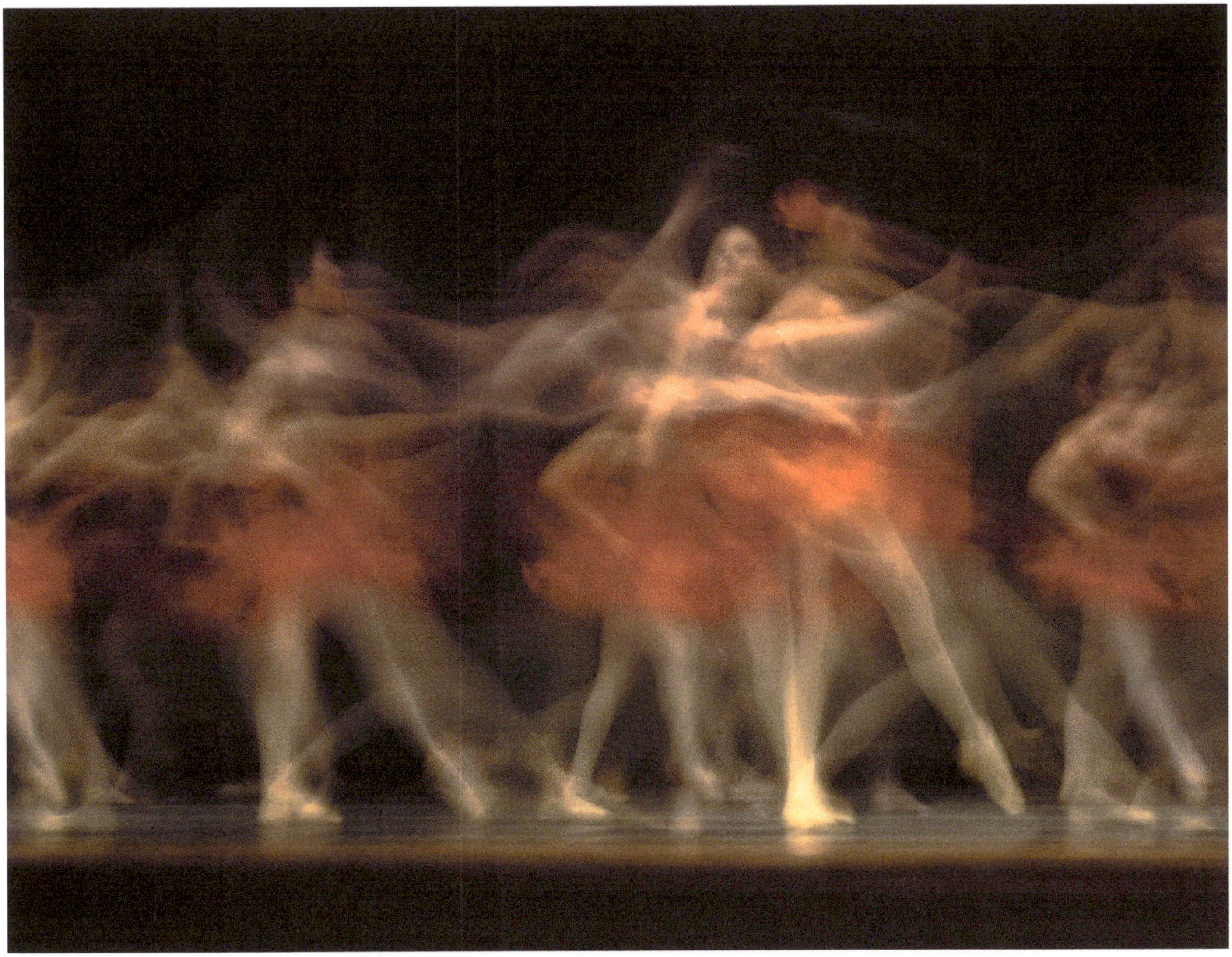

Connecting

Looking through Space

As I sit staring off into the distance,
I find myself looking at the world, but not really seeing it.

Almost as if I am trying to see through
the space, into other dimensions.

When you look through time,
you will find a way to analyze everything.

Keep looking at what you want to see
and answers will come to you.

All is there in one form or another.
Keep looking.

Space is just a form and we are all just forms of energy.

Your mind will see what it wants to.

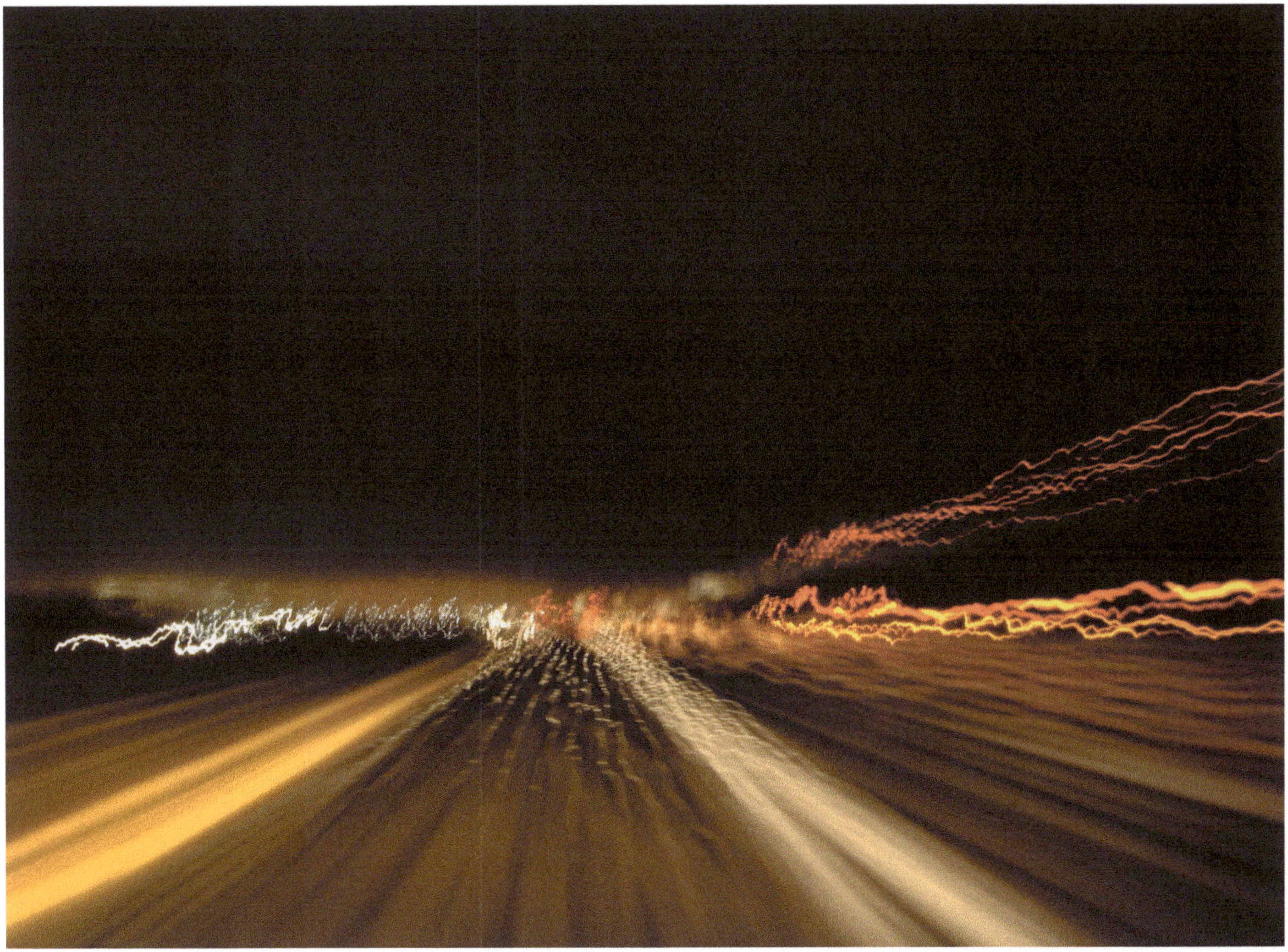

Acceptance

As I watch the cleansing smoke
from my sage, move between this world
and the one we cannot see.

I realize that its presence is there to teach us,
to accept all that is and all that you cannot see.

Even after the smoke fades,
you can still smell the fragrance.

Connecting Worlds

Chills once again overtake my body.

It is this knowing... that my world is
connecting to the other.

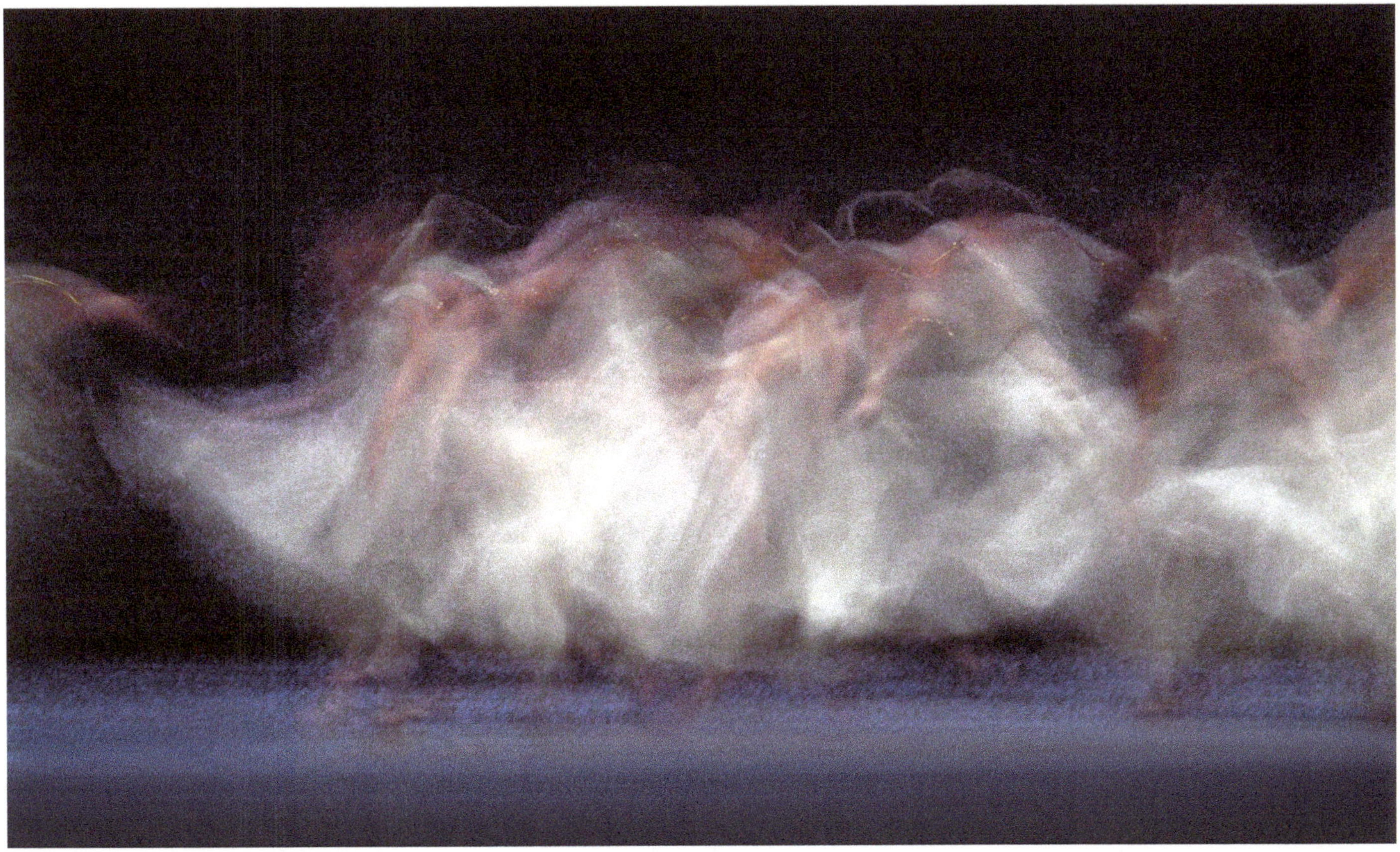

Tingling

My body feels the tingling,
whenever I push my mind to reach further.

It is within this vibration, that your greatest
thoughts will come through.

The key to everything unique to you,
will unfold very quickly when you are in this state.

There is always a connection to be felt.

When you have this connection…
all forces are working together to bring you
to your great potential.

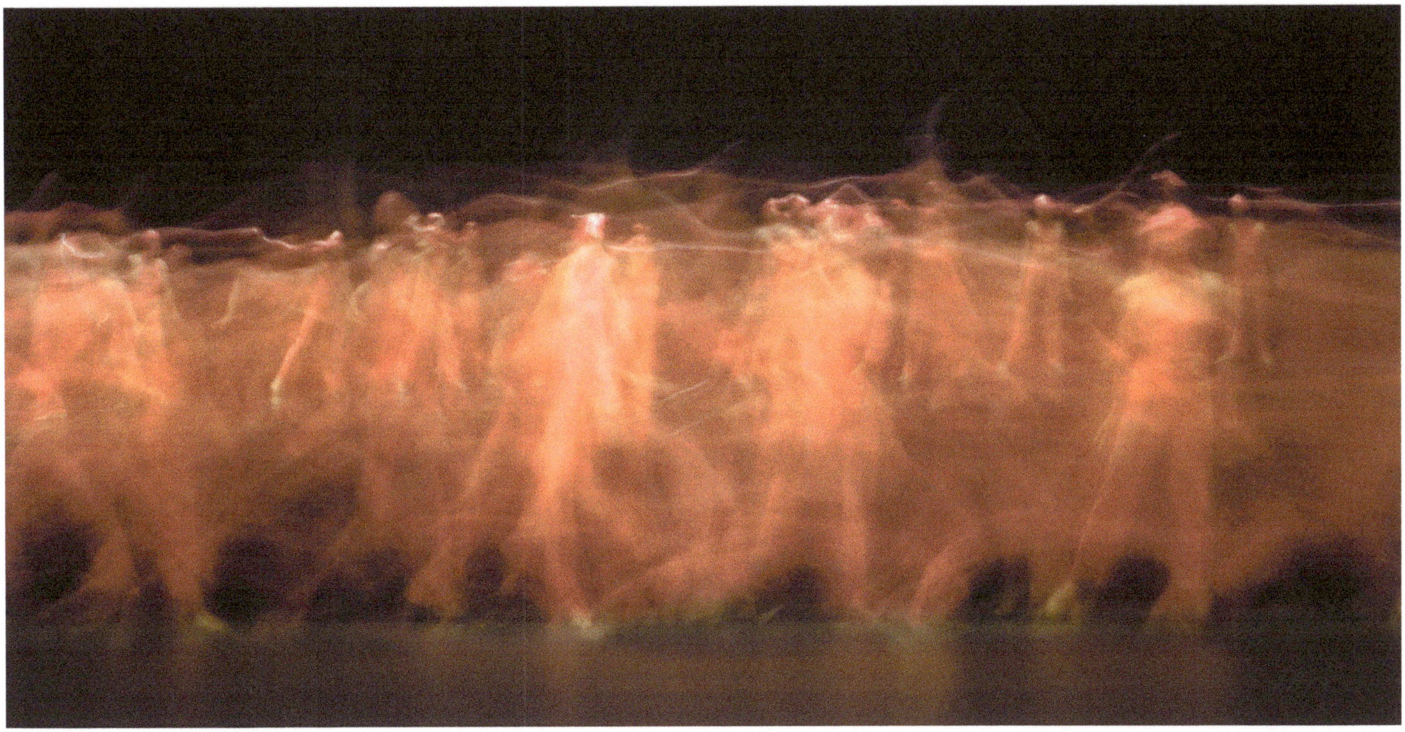

Connectivity

An excitement courses through me,
when I feel the energy flow through my body.

I feel myself floating on connectivity.

Learn to ride the waves of connection,
through this energy vibration.

My thoughts can take me wherever I want to go.

You have the ability to connect to infinite distances.
All that ever was and is to be… is before you.

Take all that you need...
It is yours.

Thank you.

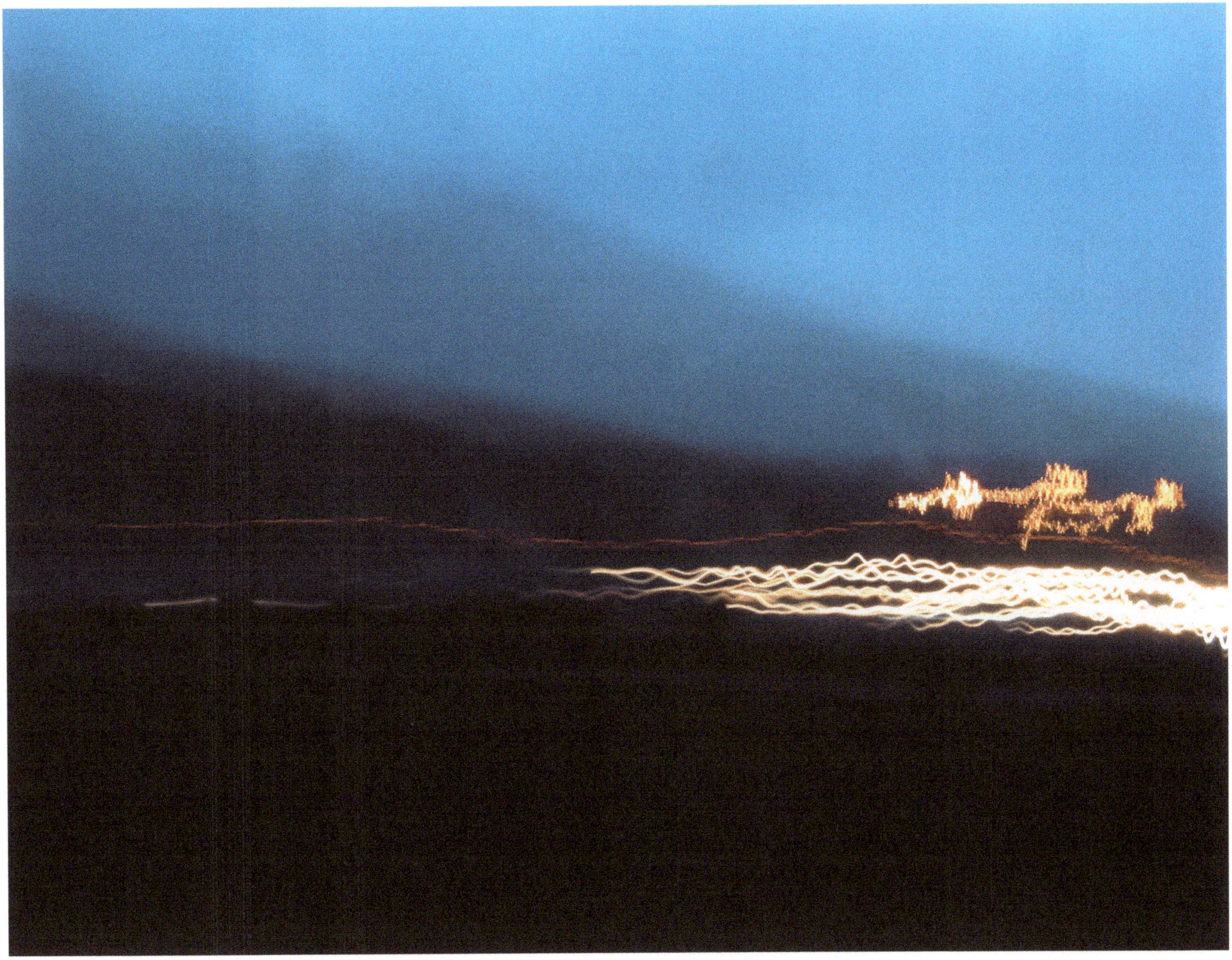

Love

My Love

One cannot put a measure on my love for you.

It is a love that grows stronger and stronger each day.

It is a love that intensifies itself deep inside my heart...
never having or wishing to part.

It is a love that will remain true as long as one can see...
and this love, can come from only me.

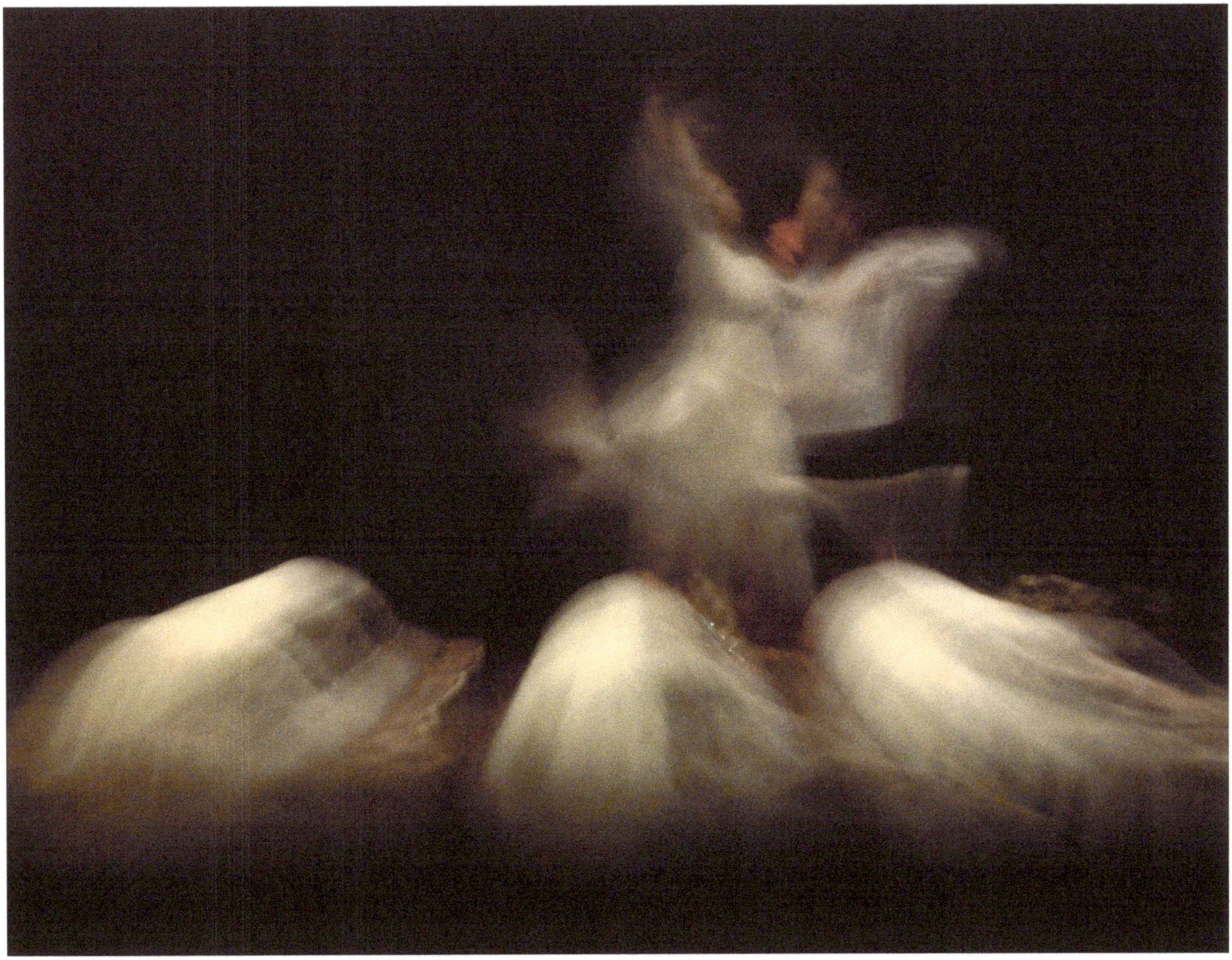

Love is a Gift

Why am I so lucky to have found such an
amazing partner to travel through life with?

All good things come to those who put forth effort.

*You cannot live a healthy life, if there is no
effort put forth in keeping what you believe in.*

*All good will come,
when you go forward knowing...
that to love,
is a gift that you should not take for granted.*

Friendship

Friendship is like a diamond.

There are many facets just waiting to be discovered.

All can shine bright, if you accept all parts.

The strength and resilience of your diamond,
is always there to remind you of what you have.

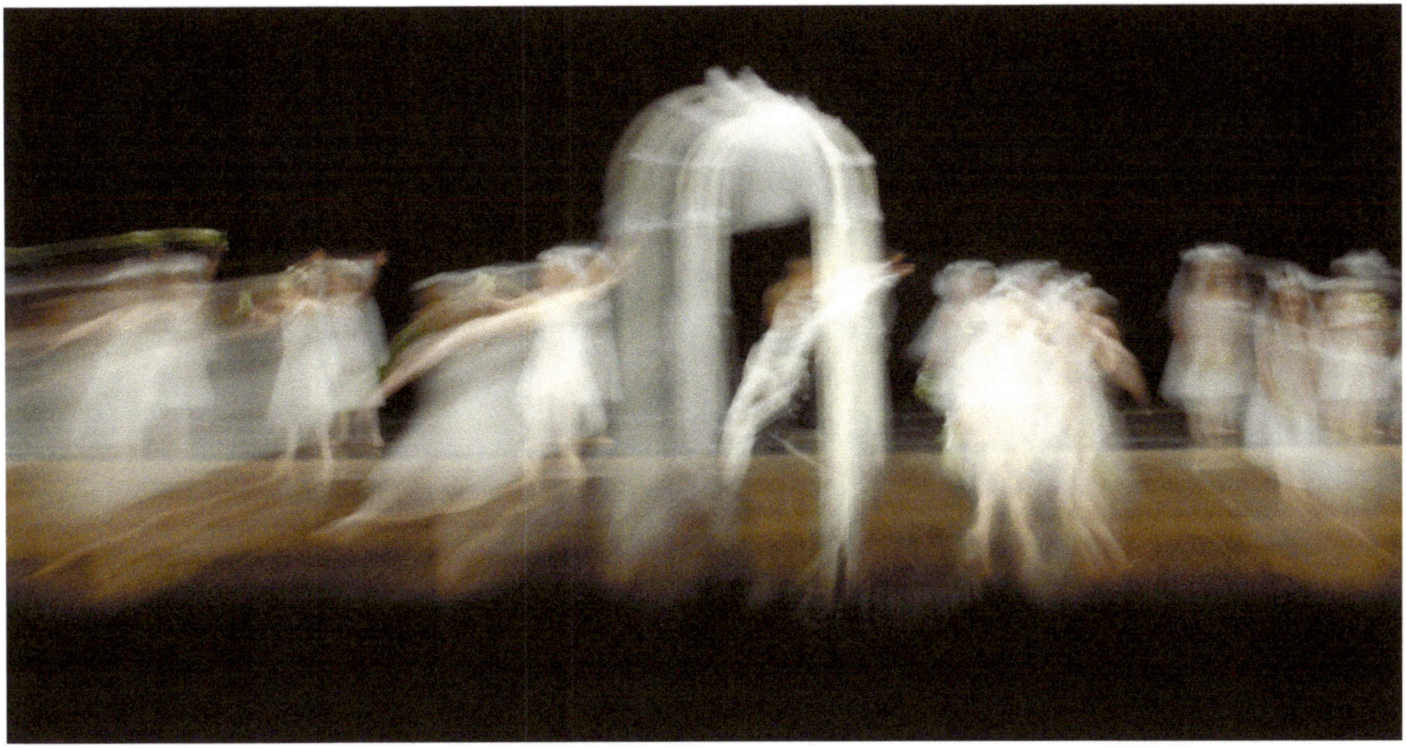

Open Heart

Love is what happens when you open your heart.

It is not something that can be taken away… ever.
It will always be with you.

Listen for all signs.

Love is always there… in nature, in people, in everything.

Hear…
All signs point to love.

Know that everywhere… there is love.

Love is what drives this world, if people would listen.

Lead with an open heart and all is possible.

Perception

Love can be everything or nothing…
It is all in how you perceive it.

Follow with an open heart and you will be
led to what your great potential is.

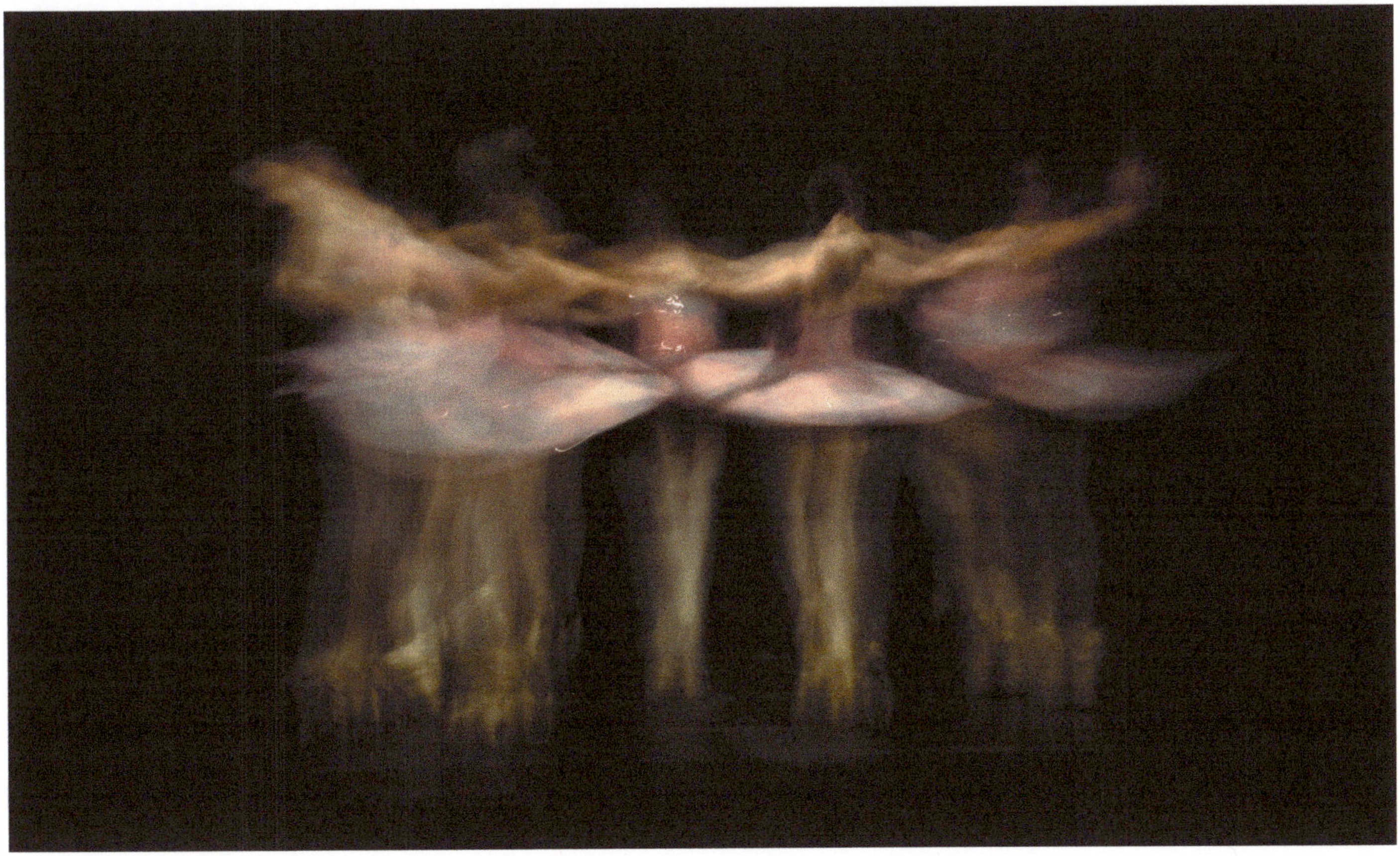

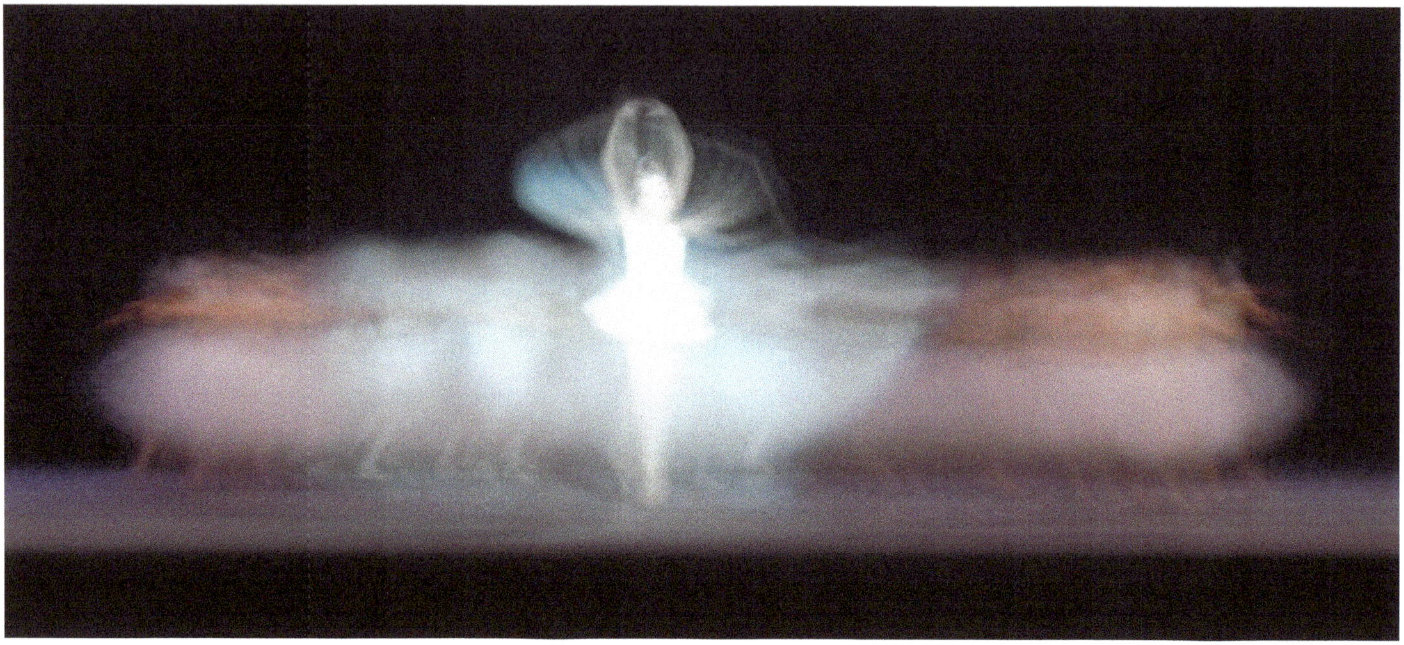

We are all We Need

Do we, need other people; or are we, all we need?

You, are all you need.

You need to be able to make yourself happy…
Then the rest of the world around you will
fall into place.

The World Needs

The world needs love, peace, compassion
and
a gathering of all Souls together,
for the purpose of understanding life.

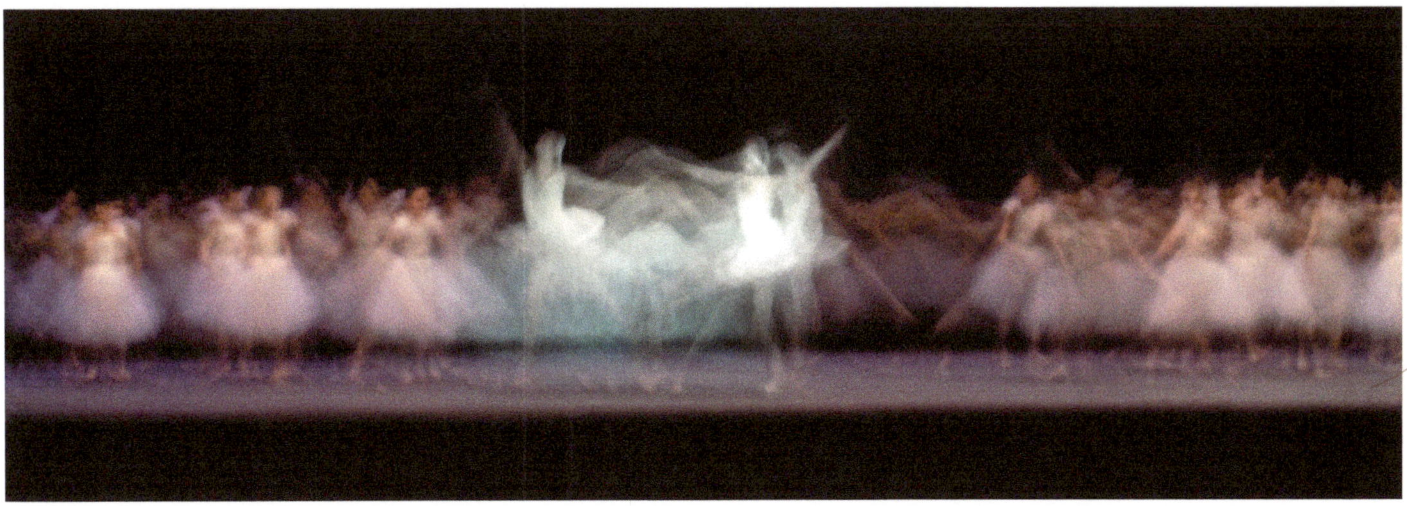

Love

Love is pure. Love is blind.
Love is an open mind.

You are in Me

You are my love.
You are my strength.
You are my life.

You are my candle when there is no light.
You are my truth when I am seeking.

You are my breath when I am tired.
You are my eyes when I cannot see.

You are my love.
You are my strength.
You are my life.

You are in me.

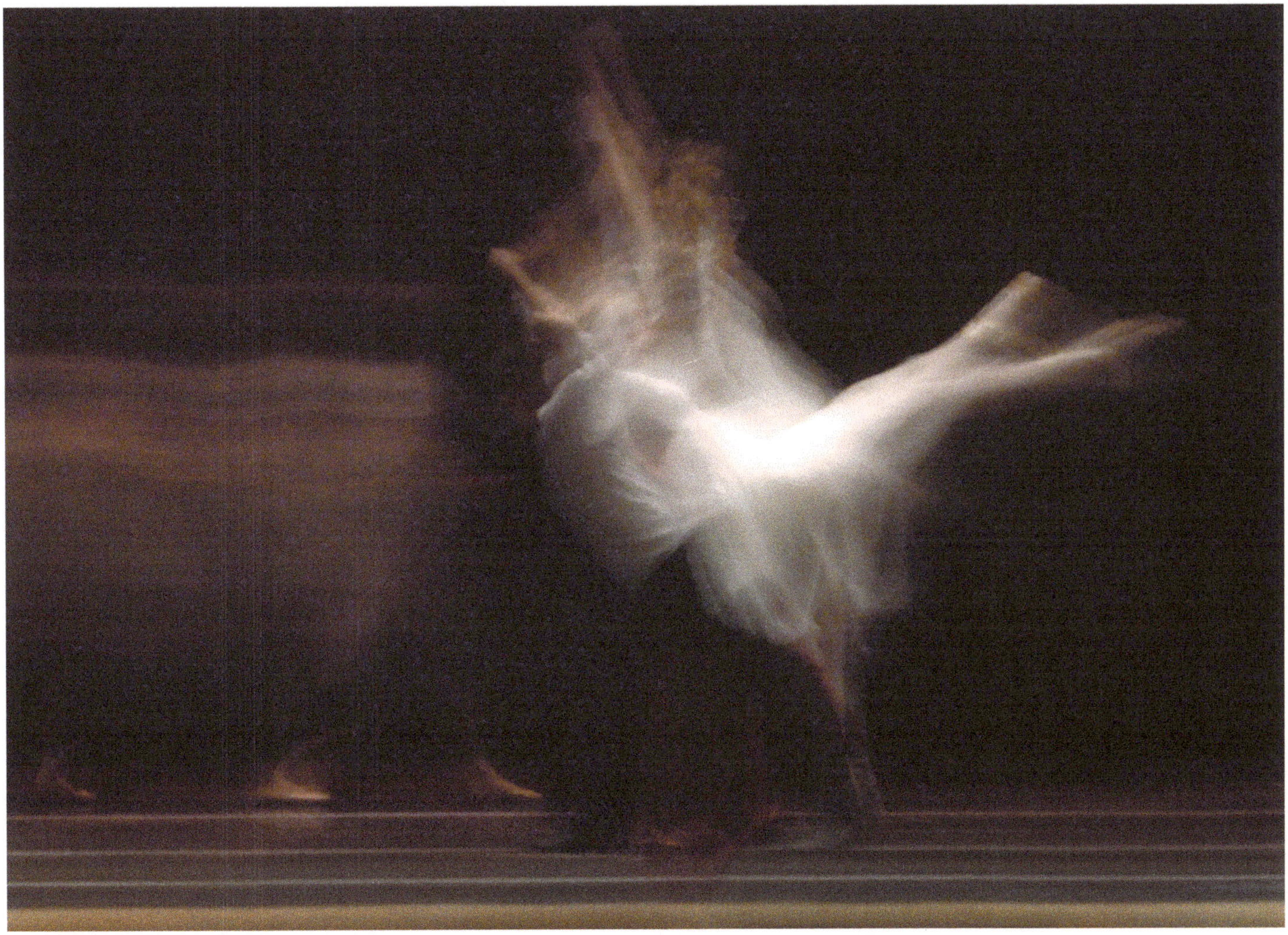

Motherhood

The biggest joy in life to me,
are my children's smiles and laughter.

When I think of how to nourish them,
my heart beats even faster.

It beats with joy and fear alike…
Am I doing things just right?

How to be the perfect mother is not an easy task.
But it is in my children's glow, that I have to bask.

Too much time, but not enough…
The days move on and on.

Am I fulfilling every dream?
I wonder, then move on.

One day I'll get to untouched dreams,
when the time is right.

But for now my dreams lie sleeping,
in their beds upon this night.

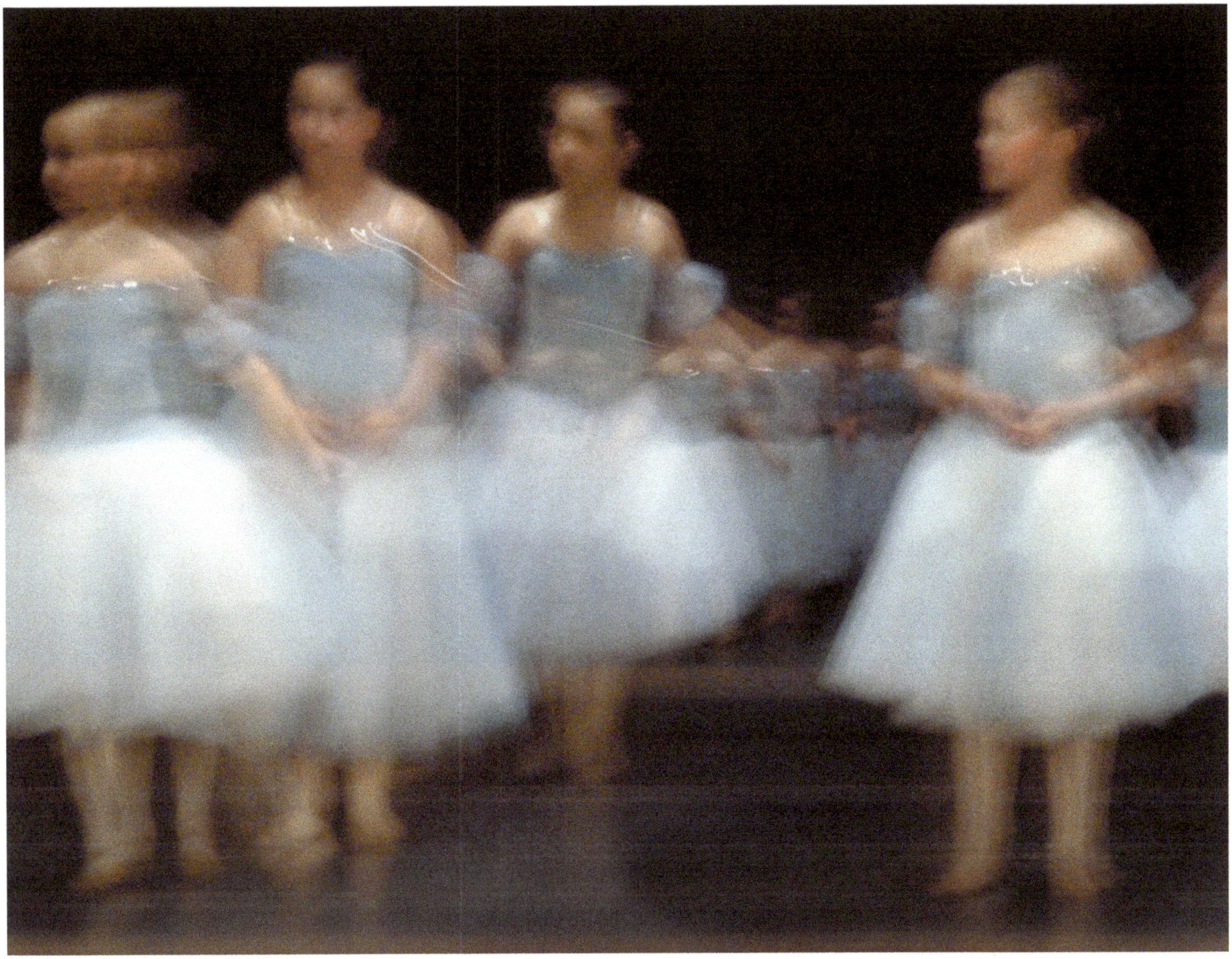

Our Beach

Our life together is like this very special beach of ours.
The beach where we began our journey
through life together.

It started out perfect in every way, untouched by time.
But slowly and surely the sands of time took over
and changed the face of the beach.
But only in appearance,
for the real feeling of this beach will always be perfect.

Just as we go through time together,
our appearance may change,
along with our goals and directions…
But our love always remains constant,
like the tide, never ending.

Some days calm and clear, other days rough
and challenging… but then calm again.
Each day, molding and shaping our beach… our love.
Changing... but always constant.

Some days all we can see and feel,
are the rocks hard beneath our skin.
But a new day arises and the soft, warm sand fills our hearts.
What a blessing to be able to ride the tides of life
and to have a partner to share the feelings,
of the hard rocks and the soft sand.

There would be a lifeless feeling without the changing tide.
Our Love and our beach also bring a strong feeling of security.
No matter how many separate paths we take in life,
the sands are always there, perhaps a little changed…
but always there.

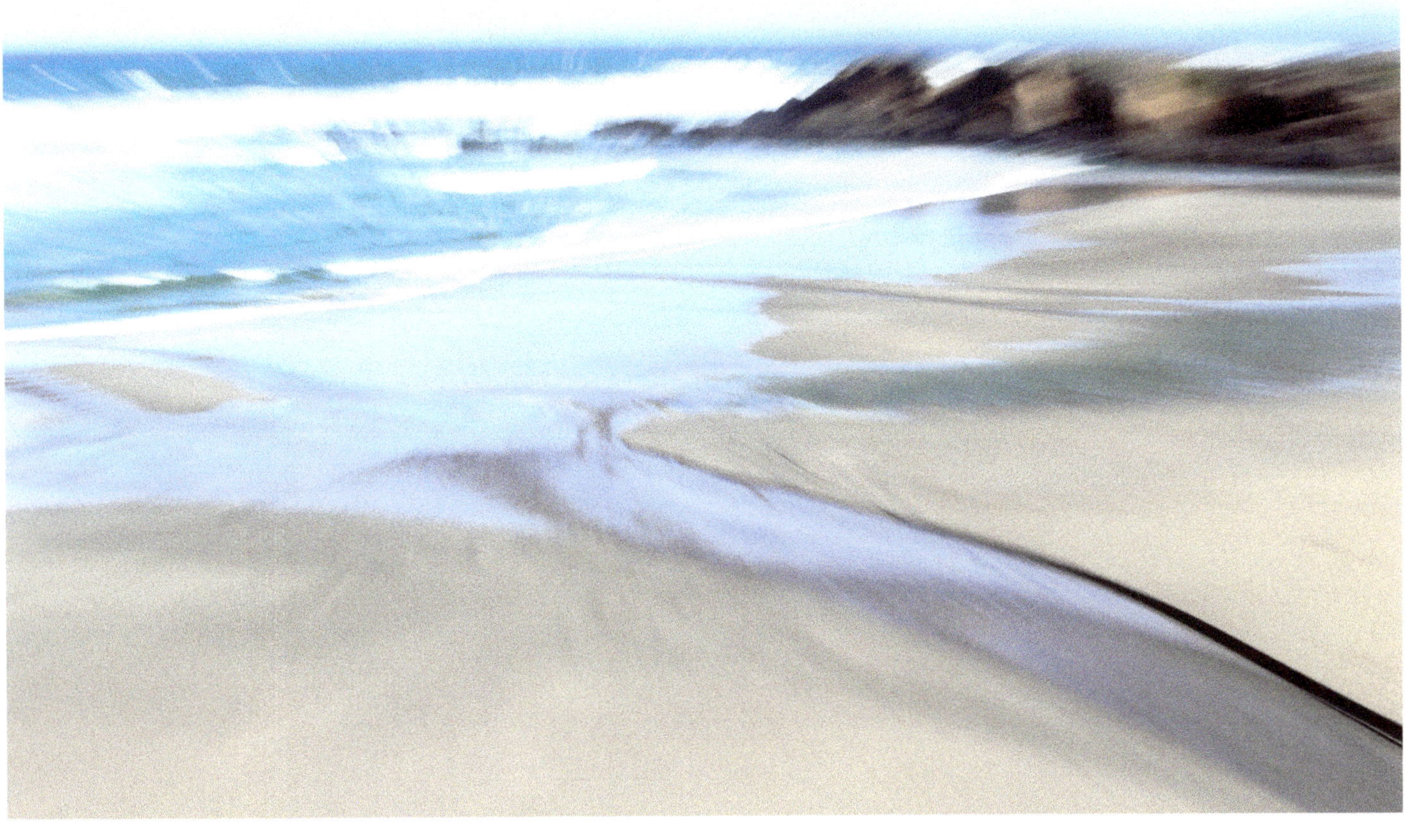

How reassuring to know that when the tide goes out,
it always comes back in.

We are very lucky to have found each other in life and
to have our beach to come back to and represent our love.

Constant, changing and never ending!

Passing Storms

Passing Storm

When I am able to stop
and listen to life…

Worlds come alive
that were once invisible.

As I fully embrace the experience
of the nature storm in front of me,

I can see the renewal of life happening.

The trees stand tall not even shaken.

They are wise in knowing that the
storm always passes…

leaving their roots nourished
in preparation for growth.

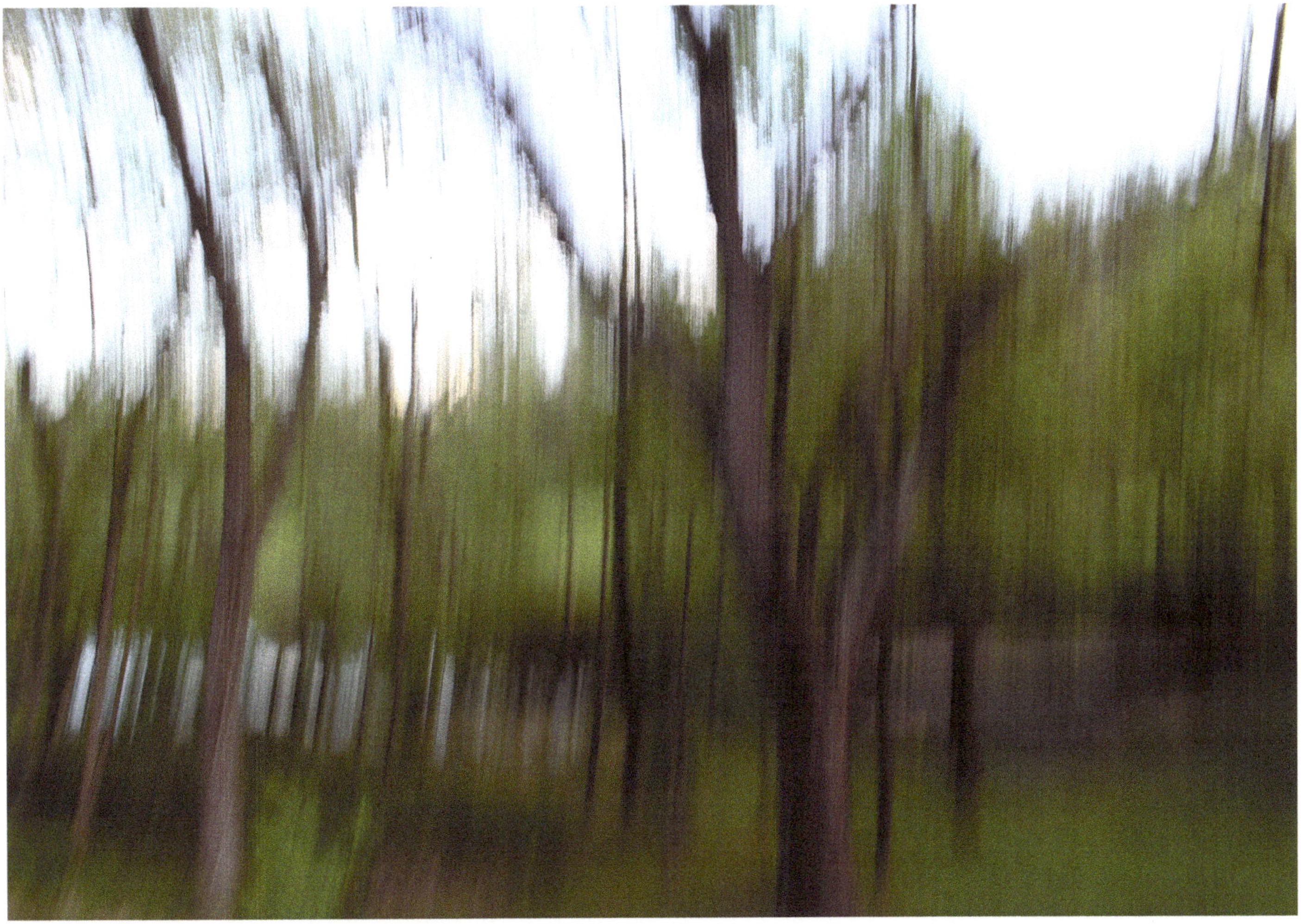

Feel your Path

No more tears in my eyes for today.
I sit and watch clouds moving by quickly.

That's how life is…
Every once in a while there is an opening in the clouds and you can see clearly.
Then as quickly as the opening comes, it closes.
The blue and white of the cloud horizon is like the mirror image of the ocean horizon.
From where ever we are in life, on earth or in the sky, everything is connected.

Life mirrors itself.
Sometimes still and then fast moving,
sometimes bright and sunny;
other times, dark and gray, then bright again.
That's one thing you can always count on…
Life is always changing.

We are all riding with the wind.
We never know where it will take us.
Imagine being a bird,
able to see life from every direction…
To flow with the wind and be comforted by the clouds white light.
We too can go to those places… in our minds.

When the eyes cannot see,
the Heart and Soul can feel.
Your instincts will take you where your destiny lies.
Our path is not always visible to our eyes.
It is our Soul that must lead us.

Feel your path… It is there.

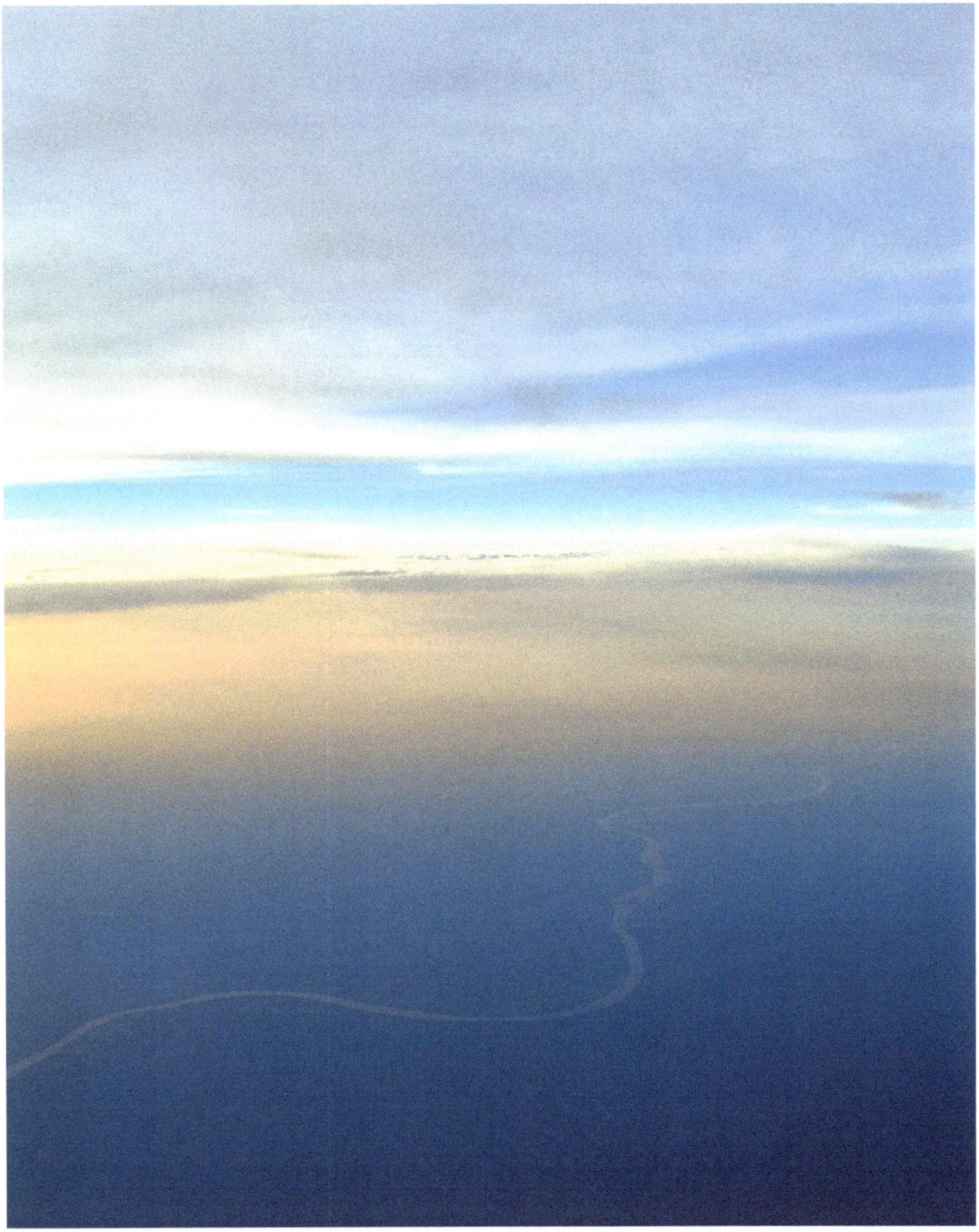

Melting Soul

I am frozen as I sit looking through
this frosted window.

In my mind, I see glimpses of truth
melting through the corners.

As life starts to chip away the outer
edges of my restless Soul,
I see a truth I did not know was there for me.

I am still, as I listen to my heartbeat
while I contemplate.

Thoughts that were once trapped in my Soul,
begin to flutter like birds in a cage…
wanting to be free.

The corners of my Soul are melting further.

One bird escapes and is free…
Oh the beauty it sees on the other side.

As it flaps its wings, the beauty and inspiration
it feels, mirrors itself back to that frosted window
and begins to melt the edges further.

One by one each bird escapes as its
inspiration is mirrored back.

There is no turning back, as each bird becomes
consumed by love.

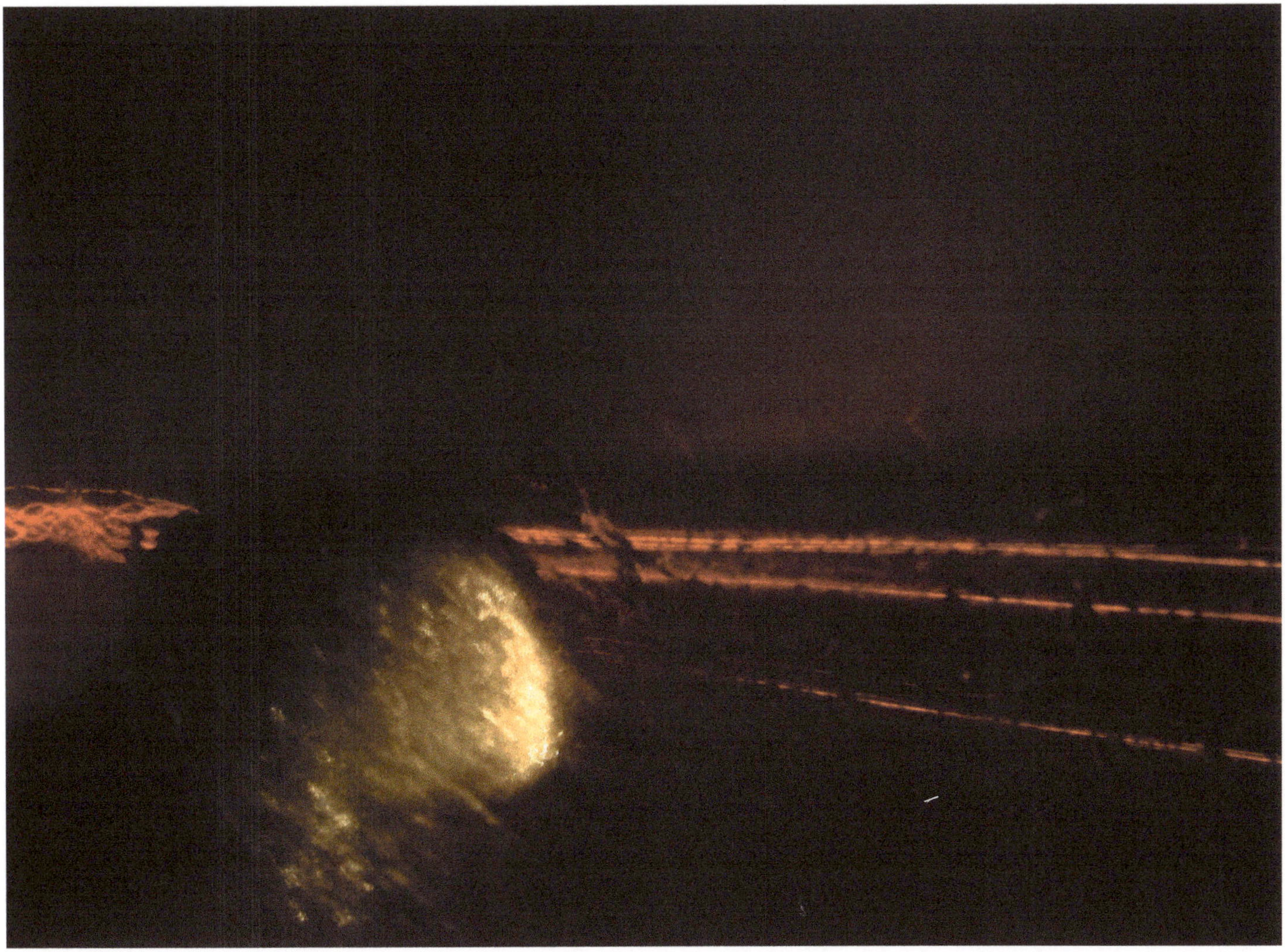

Feeling Stuck

The swirly feelings inside my Soul never stop.
They are like butterflies that never sleep,
fluttering their wings hoping for transformation.

The feelings you are feeling now,
are real and a part of you.
You need to embrace this part, to move on to the next.

It is always hard when you feel stuck…
Just know you are not going to be here forever.

Please know this.

Move forward and enjoy the life you have.

You are truly blessed with amazing gifts.
You are talented beyond belief
and can help many people…
if you will only get out of your own way.

You, are the one stopping yourself.
Please get up and move.

You can't control life...
This is a struggle that you know too well.
Please know that it is a futile trait.

Nothing can be controlled that is part of your destiny.

Release all, so you can come up with what is yours.

You cannot stay in this state… It is not serving you.
Please… everyone else is happy, you too need to be happy.

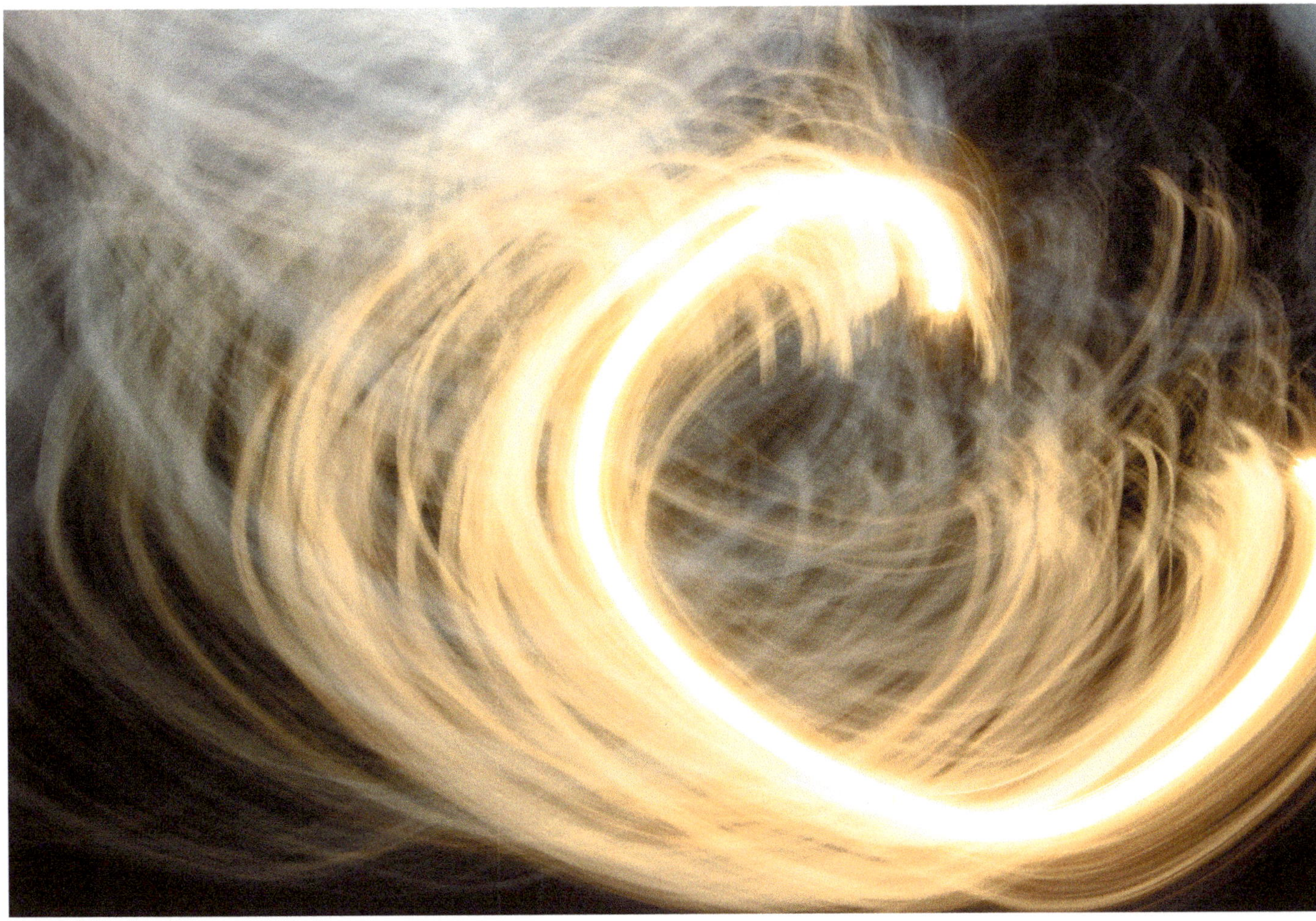

Move on

Know that what is done, is done.
You must move on to the future.

Life is always recreating itself…
Use what you learn.

Obsessive Thoughts

Living under this cloud of guilt,
is not a happy place to be.

Obsessive thoughts can and will hurt you.

*Please try to get away from the situation
when it happens.*

Go for a walk. Get outside. Change your scenery.

Loss

When you lose something,
just know to look ahead to what is coming.

Always know that there is a reason for the loss
and there will be a reason for the future.

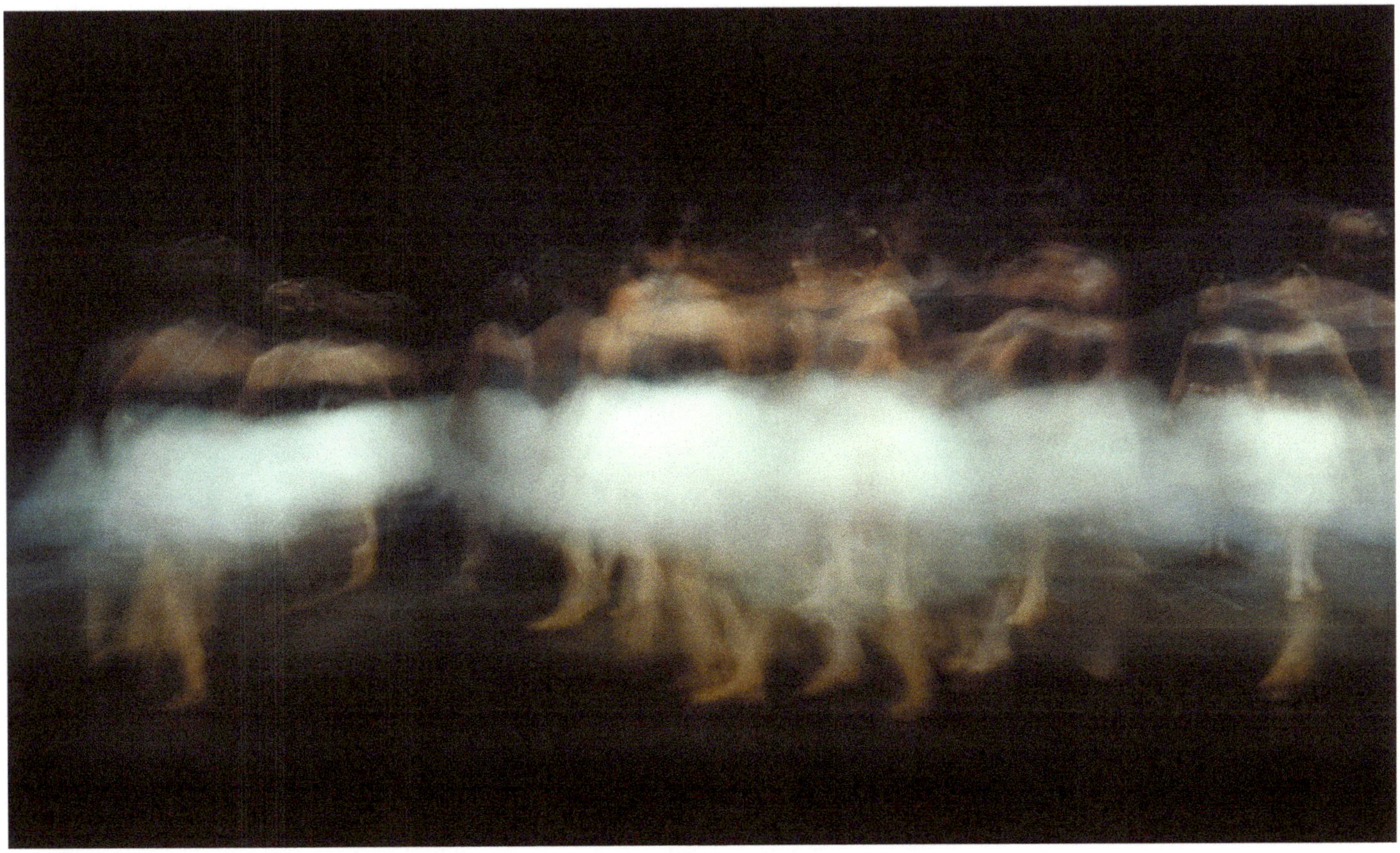

Feeling Drained

My energy feels drained in certain situations.

You can pull energy from all things around you.
Let in only what you feel will be healthy.

If you cannot change a situation,
then remove yourself from it.

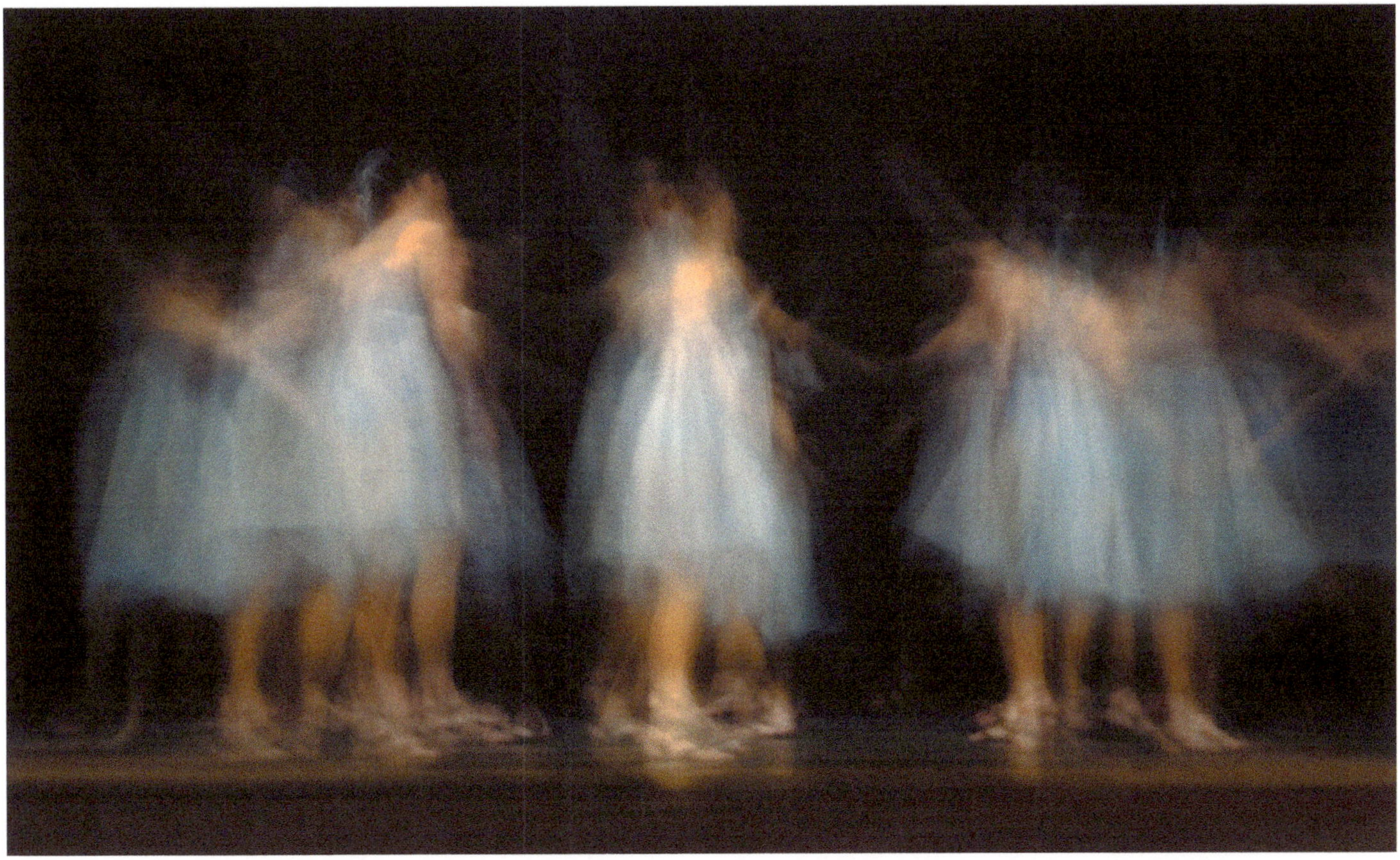

Changes

I am here, fully embracing the pain
that only comes once a month to remind me
that I am female, young and thriving.

As I approach my half century milestone,
I realize that soon I may no longer have these
bodily sensations that have been a part of me
for as long as I can remember.
As each cramp takes hold of me,
I try to savor the feeling of my youth.

As my body changes, I wonder…
Will I be as creative?
I know all too well the crazy that comes over me
as my cycle approaches.
But is it in those crazy moments that my
most creative thoughts come through?

What will happen to me as I begin to
enter into my cocoon for re-birth?

Will I come out on the other side a beautiful butterfly,
so clear in thinking that my creativity ceases?

Or, will my creativity find new ways to flutter about?

Life is always changing and everything will
come through the way it is meant to.

Different perspectives will be given to you…
Age can bring on new ways of looking at things.

You will be so amazed at your new thought processes.
All will be amazing as it happens.

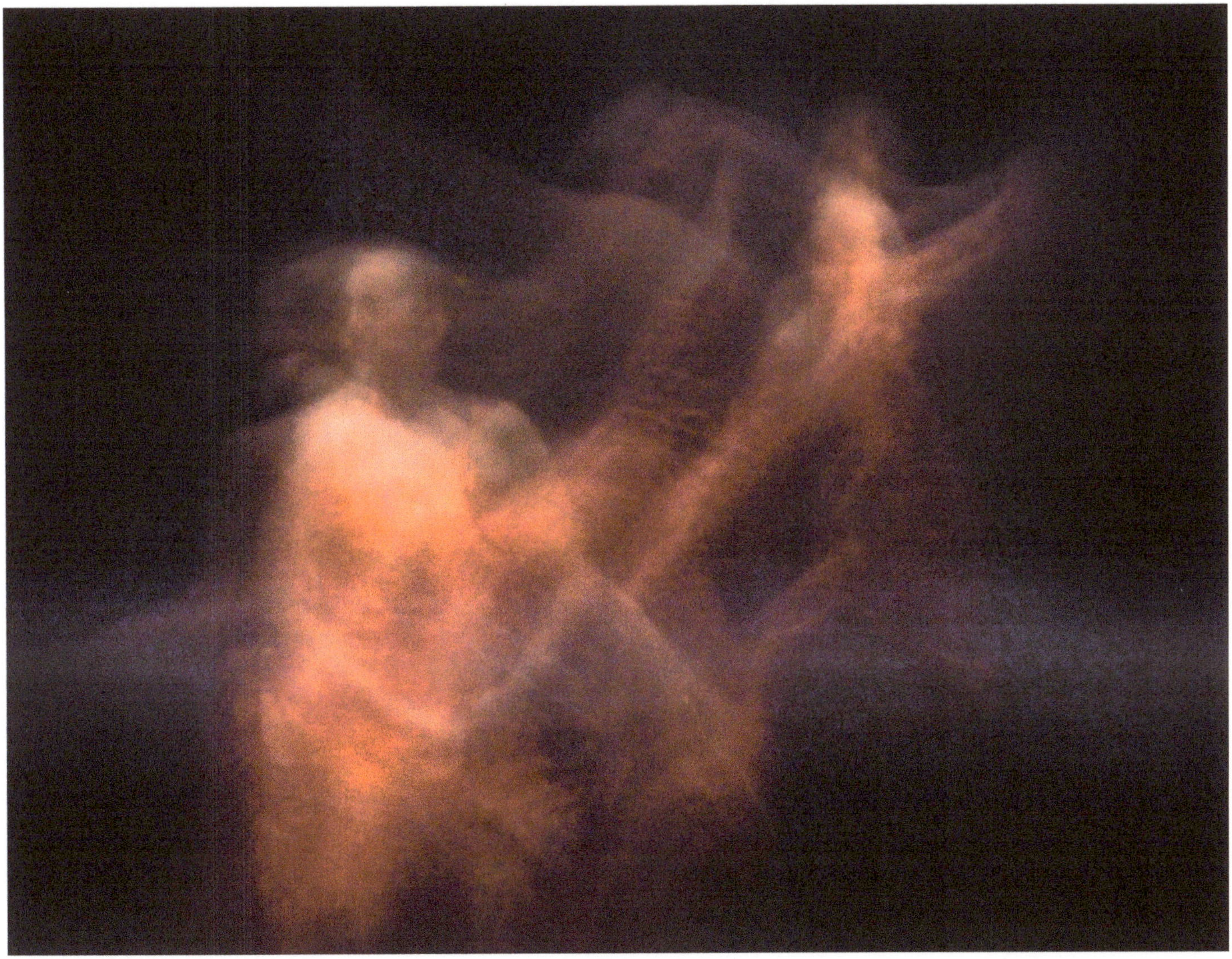

Prisoner in my Mind

One by one, the overwhelming thoughts
in my mind take control of me.
They weaken my Soul and keep me captive.

I am a prisoner in my own mind.

My Soul holds the key to the door, but won't let me use it.
It knows that I can only be free when my mind is willing.

When I breathe, I feel the union
between my Soul and mind... slowly the door opens.

As quickly as the light peers through,
my mind feels anxious and retreats back into the dark.

What is in the dark that is so appealing to my mind?

From in the dark, my mind builds pathways
that are comforting and clear.

But my Soul's light is stronger than the dark...
My heart wants to follow the path led by my Soul.

As I breathe, I look around and there is no door.

My Soul is free once again.

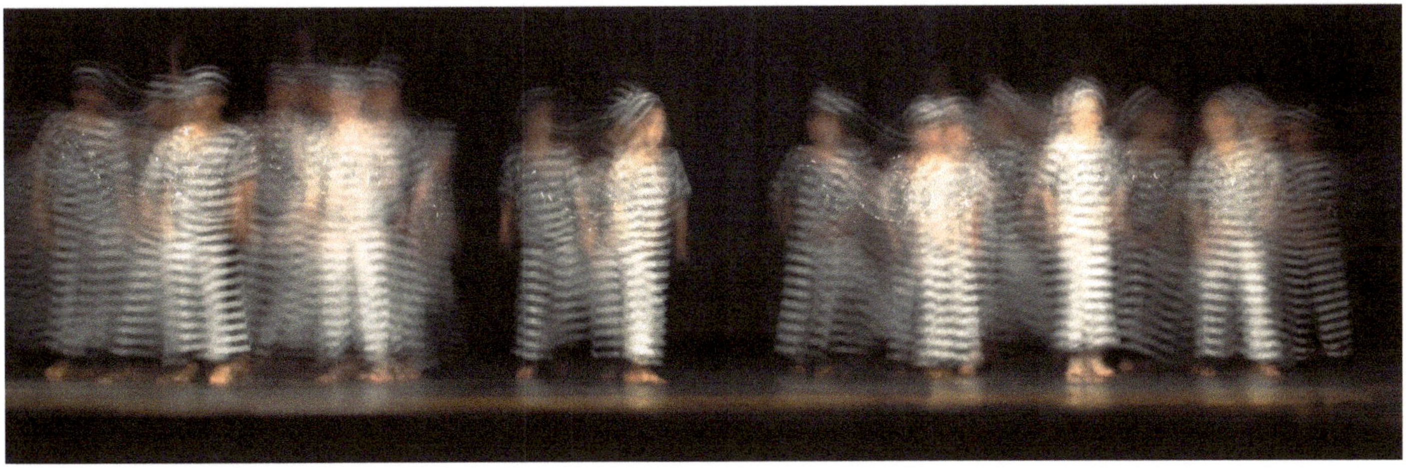

Embrace Yourself

It is in these moments
when my heart feels heavy,

that I am able to go into the
dark side of my soul.

Your soul is made up of many parts.
All are useful.

Just trust that to understand
all of who you are...

you need to embrace
all of who you are.

One by one,
pieces will come together
and your truth will become clear.

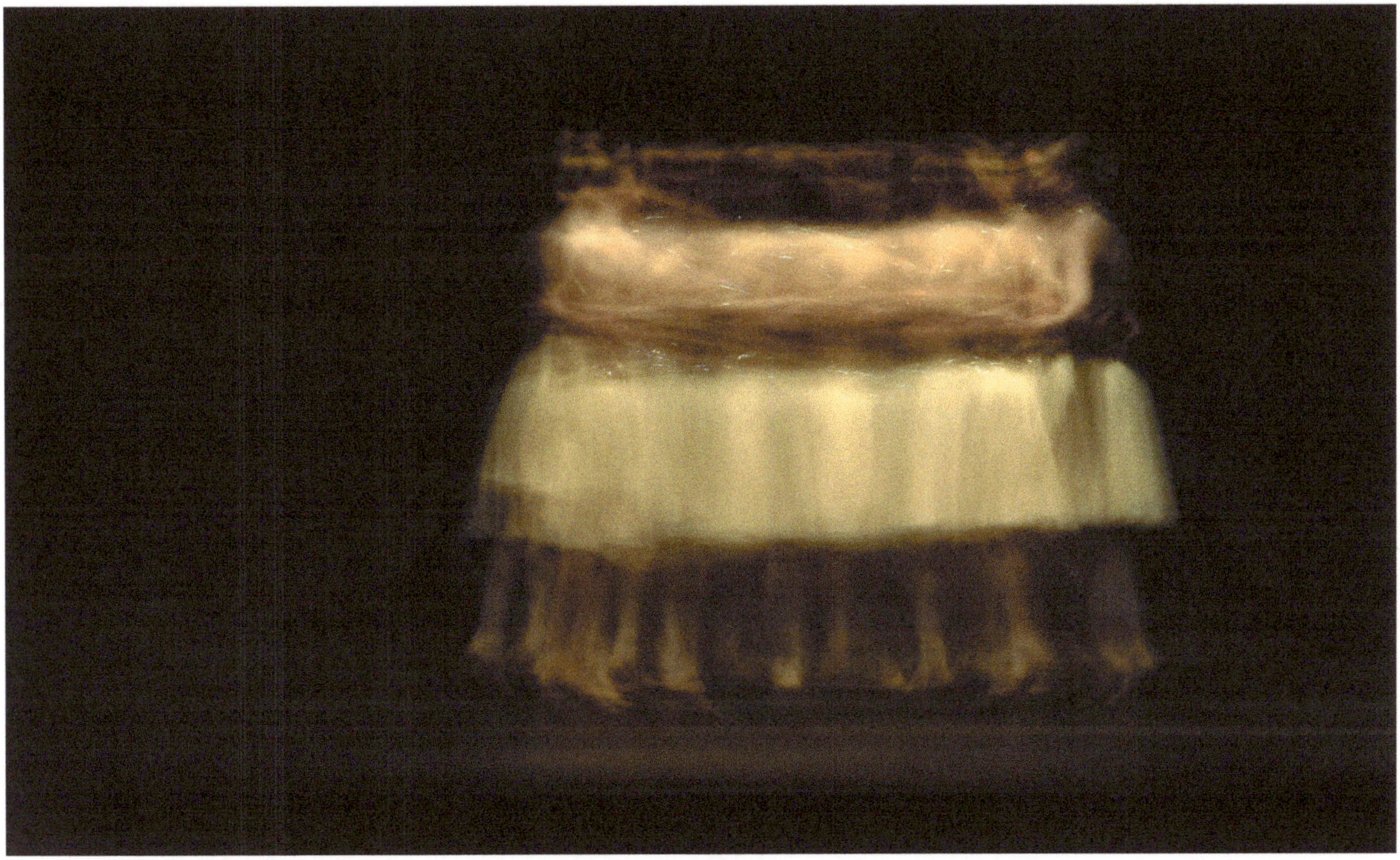

Dark to Light

Dark to Light

I feel a calm that only comes
after the storm.
A renewed sense of inspiration fills my Soul.

Why is it that we must move through
the dark,
to be able to see the light?

Life is filled with dark… but the light is always there,
maybe not always visible.

You need to forge through with a knowing,
that the light will always be there to carry you.

Never doubt the force of light.
It will come through in all situations…
You just have to know where to look.

Be able to see, what is in front of you.

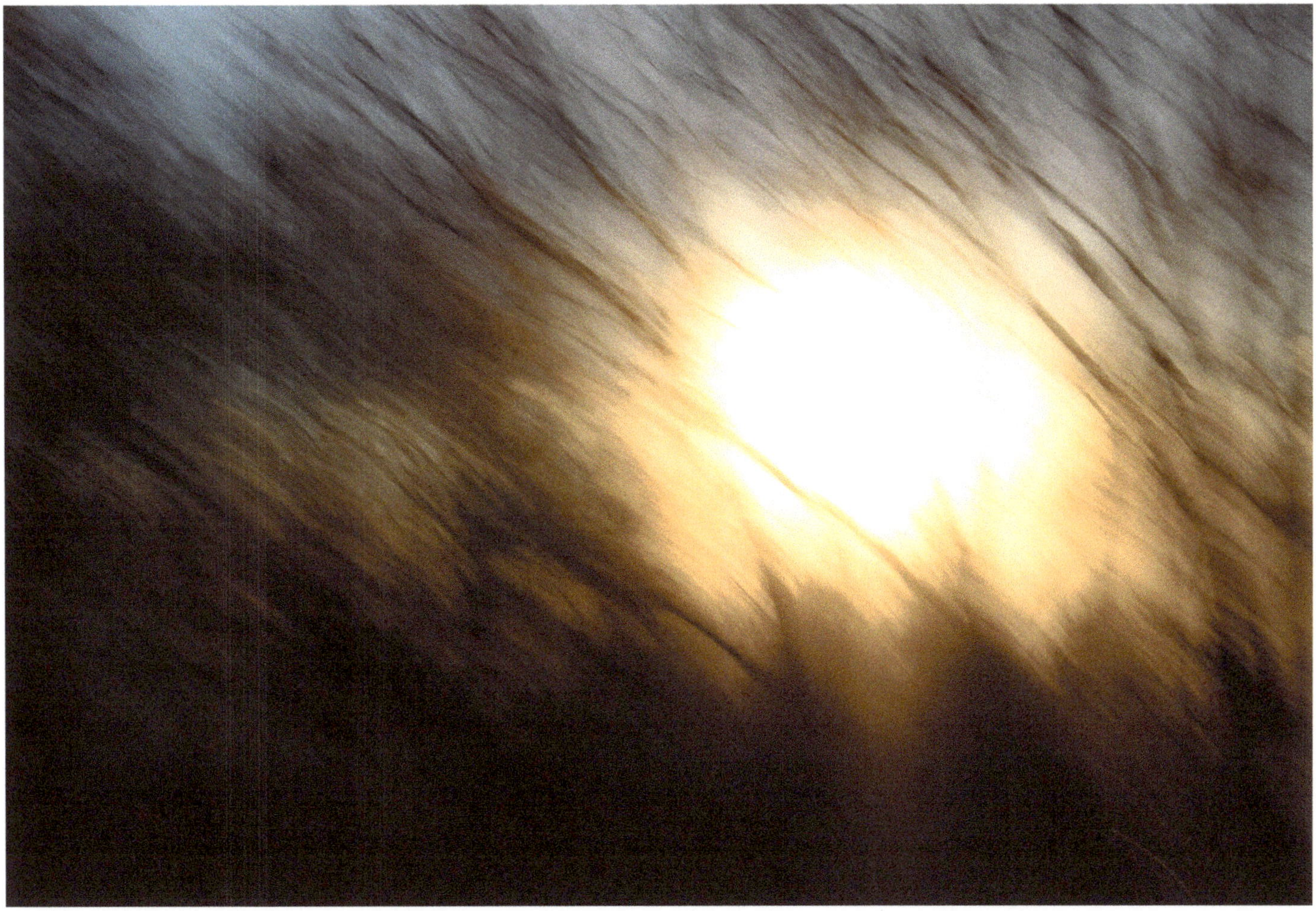

Reflections

The sun reflects off of the airplane wing
and hits my eyes.

The light is so bright I cannot see past it.
I see floating orbs through my glasses.

I contemplate all that lies behind the brightness,
that I am not allowed to see.

In life, we always say we should live in the light…
But what if that light is so powerful that we cannot
begin to see what is there for us?

Is that why we must close our eyes… to fully
appreciate the magic behind the light?

Going in deep, behind closed eyes will let us explore
the world we cannot see with our eyes open.

It is all there for us…
You just have to know where to look.

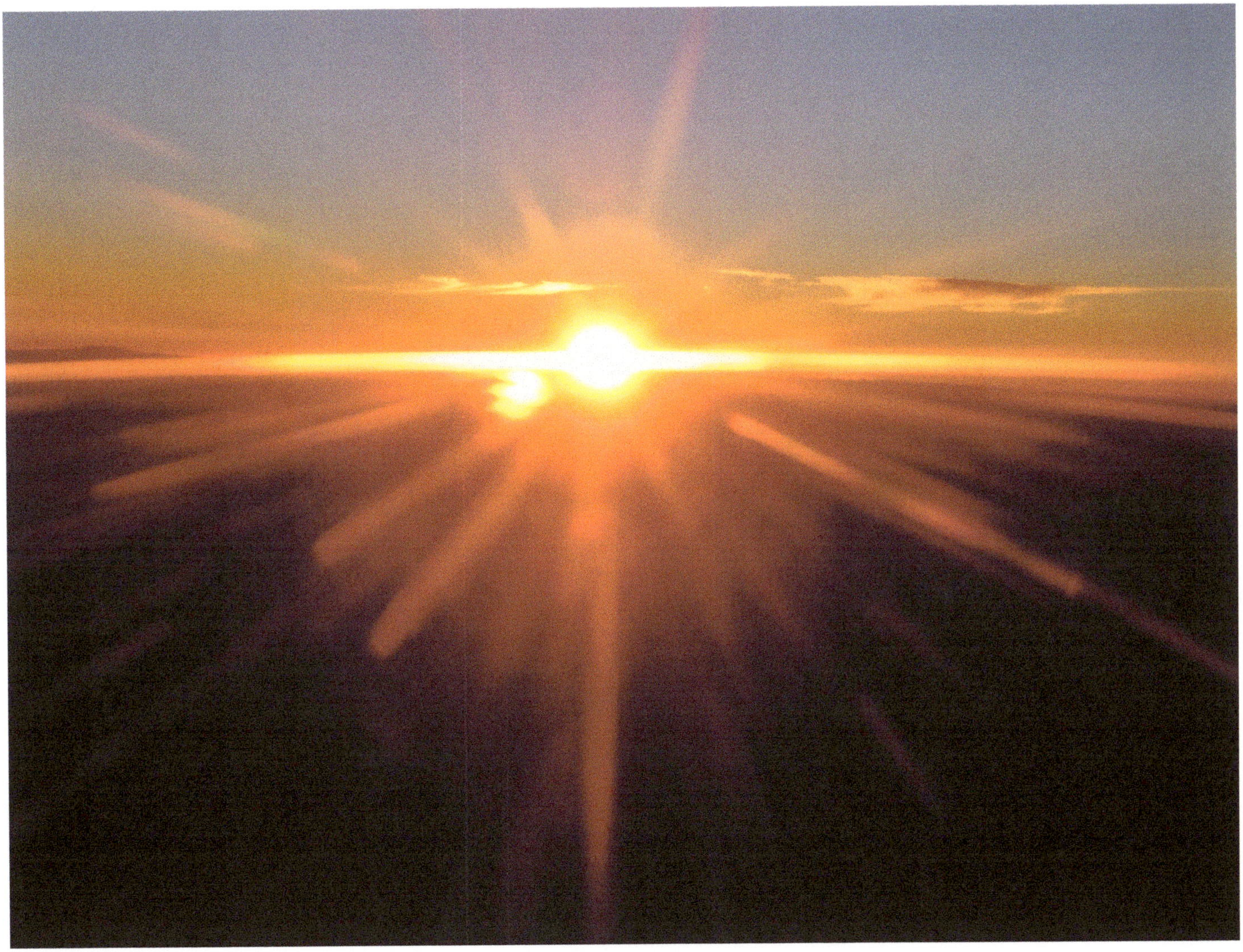

Closed Eyes

With open eyes, I can see only
what is immediately in front of me.

But by closing my eyes...
I can see infinite possibilities.

I can see the Universe in all its vastness.

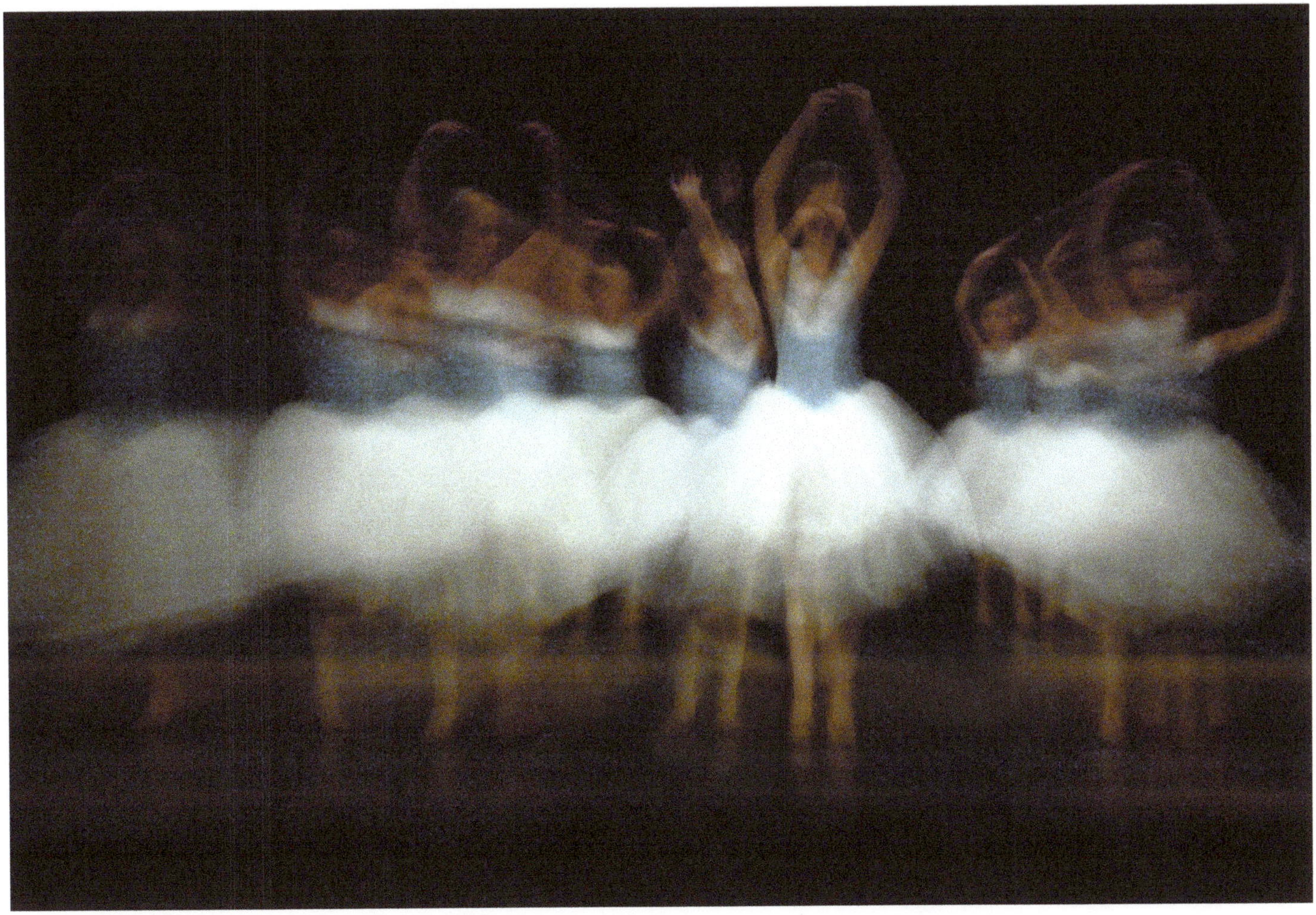

Hidden Parts

Hidden within your drawers,
there are things used and unused.

It is like the Soul…
There are many parts that you have control over
and many you don't.

Just trust that with a clear mind… you can reach all parts.

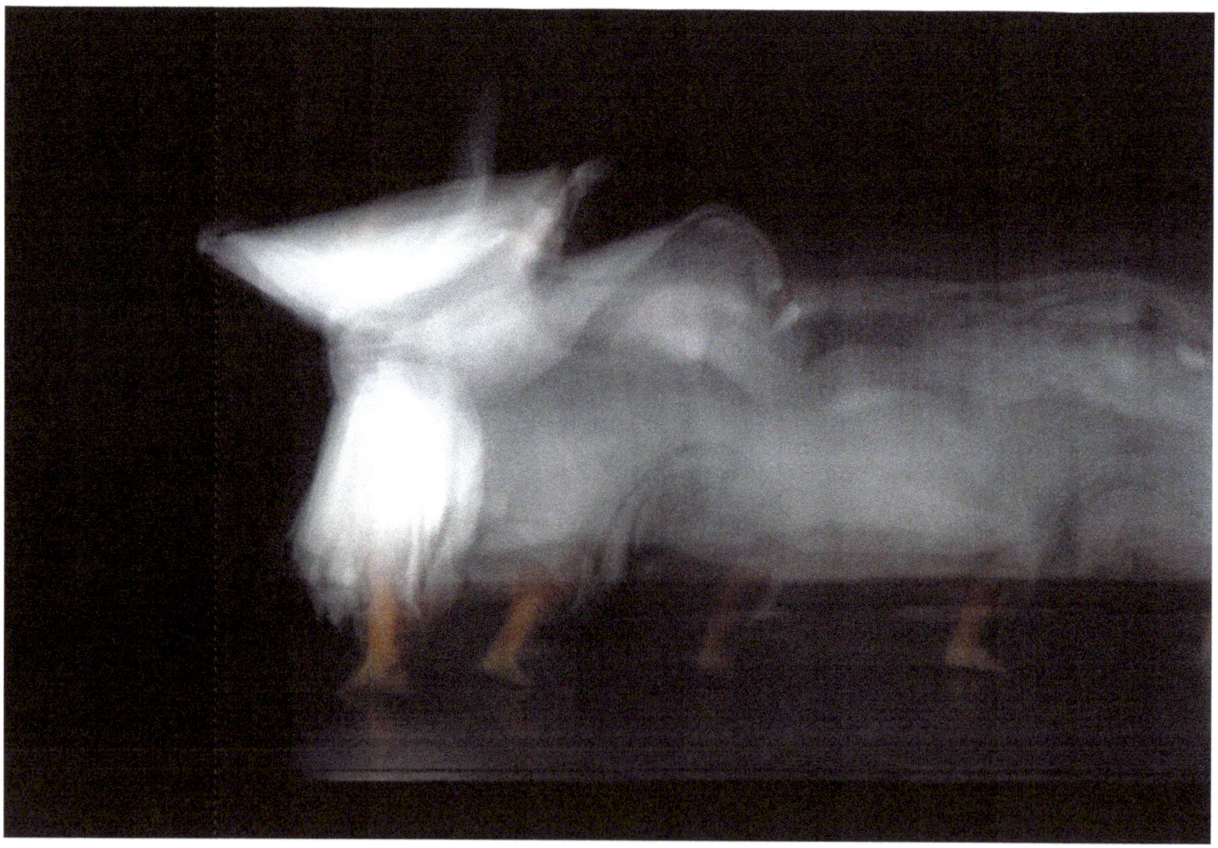

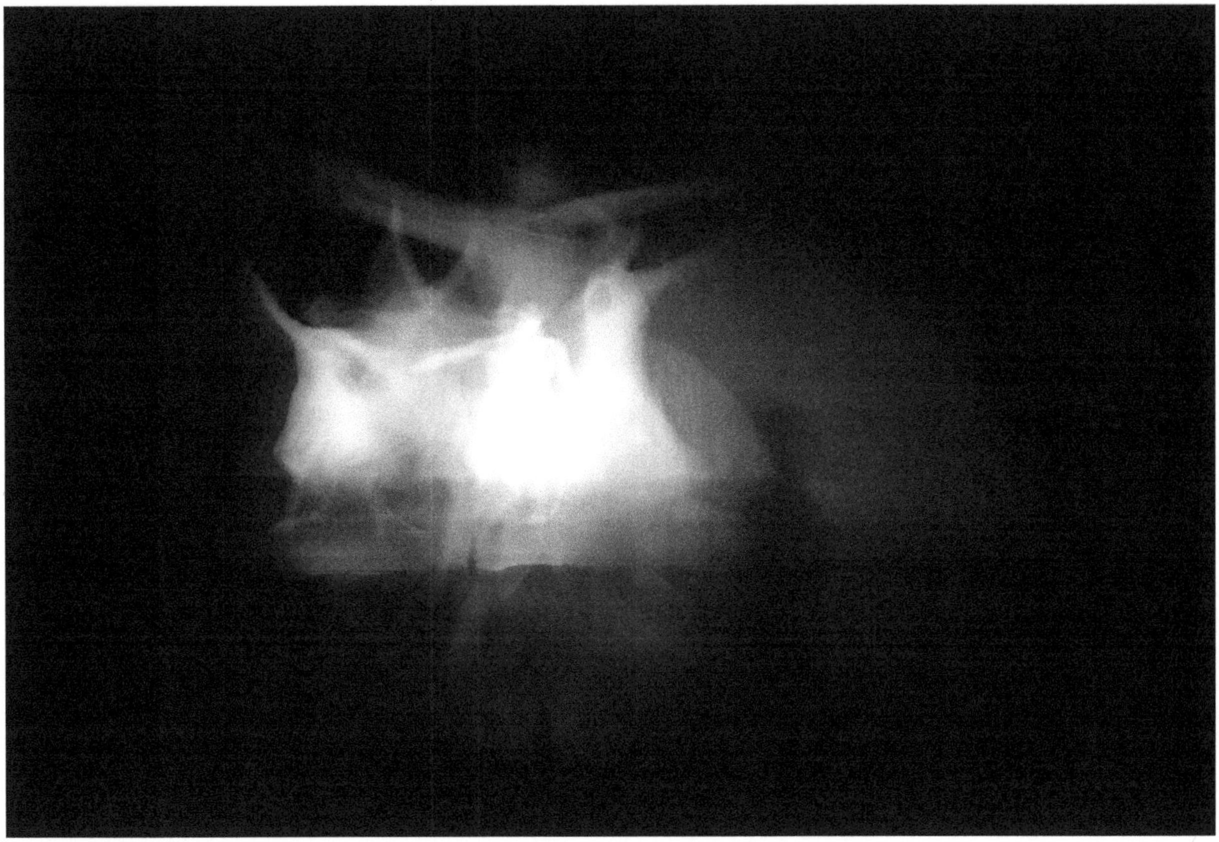

Shining Soul

When we live in the light...
our shadow becomes illuminated.

It is in this spotlight, that our Soul can shine.

See the Light

As I sit calmly and listen for the breath
of my Soul,

I close my eyes and it is dark.

I embrace the darkness and realize,

that it is only from within the darkness…
that you can see light.

Greatest Strength

Embrace the dark side of your Soul…

It is within these imperfections that our
greatest strengths lie.

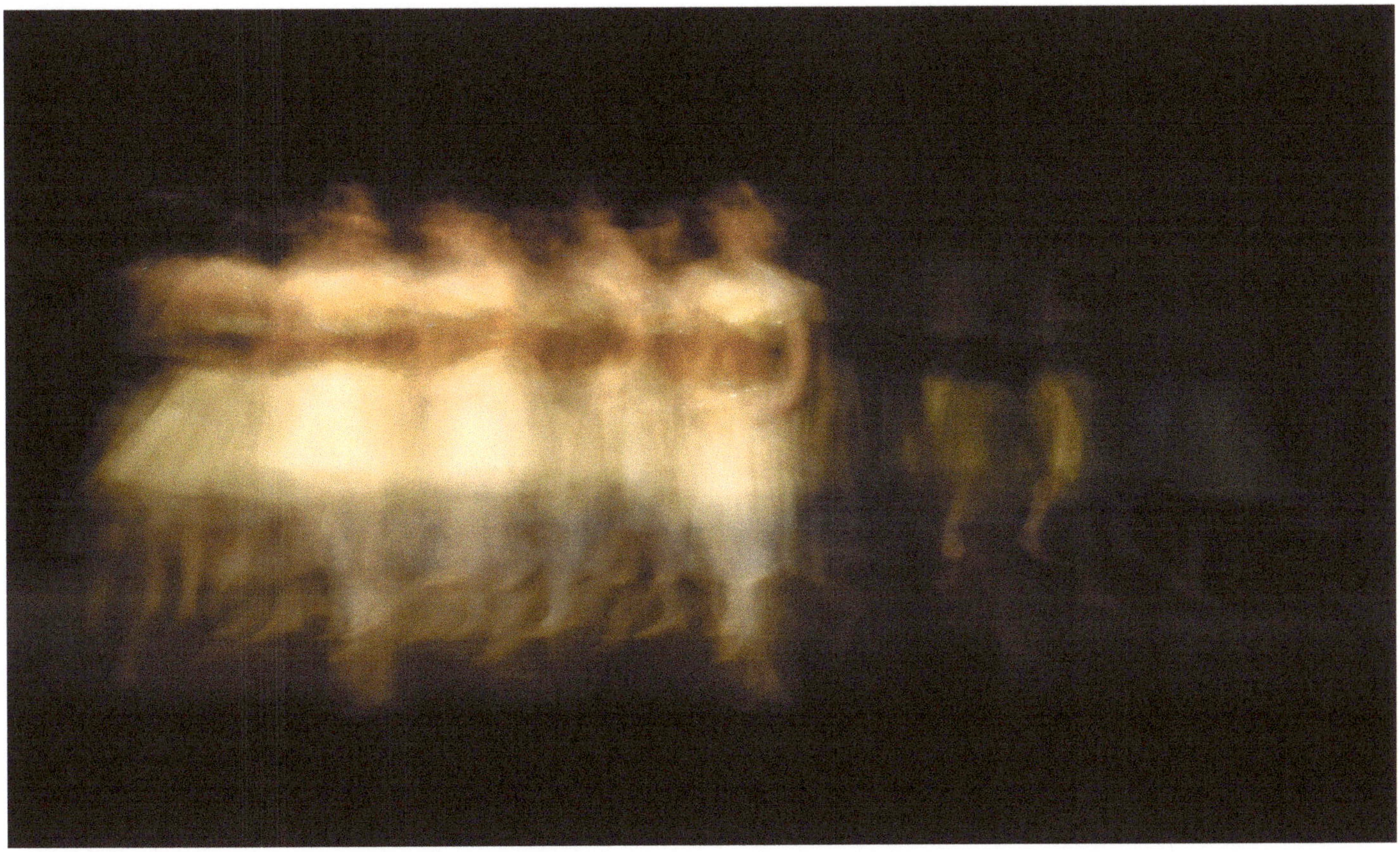

Clarity

As the sun begins to rise,
I see the outline of the dark trees
against the deep blue sky.

When we let in the light…
we are able to see with great clarity.

Ever so slowly the sky begins to brighten
and the trees become more visible.

A new day is starting.

Release

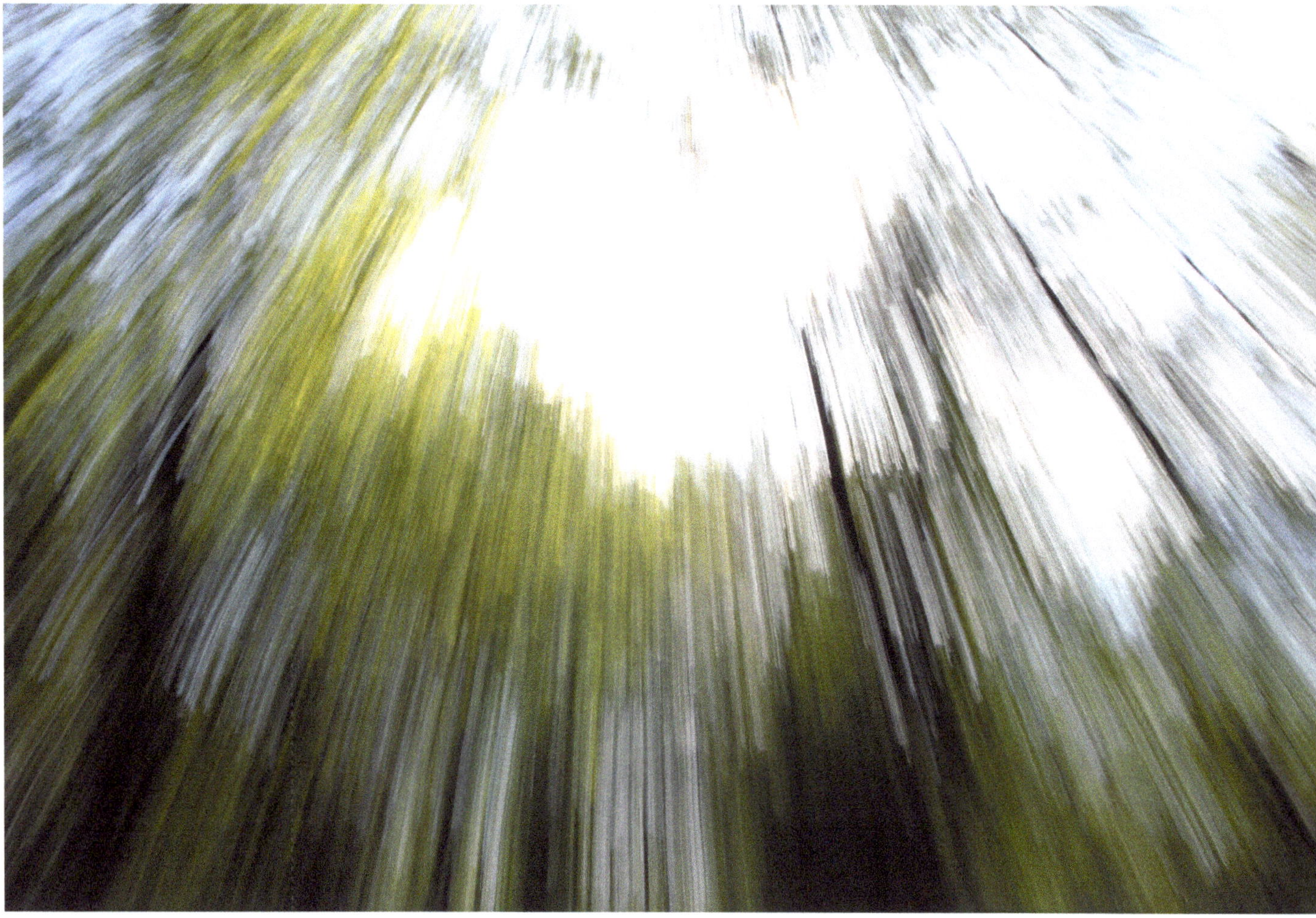

Release

As the clouds release its precious rain…
flowers are encouraged to bloom.

We too must release what is no longer needed.
By doing so… we encourage our Soul to bloom.

Constant Flow

Each droplet of rain falls,
with the assumption that the other drops will follow.

Life cannot be stopped... it is a constant flow.
Open your heart and become part of that flow.

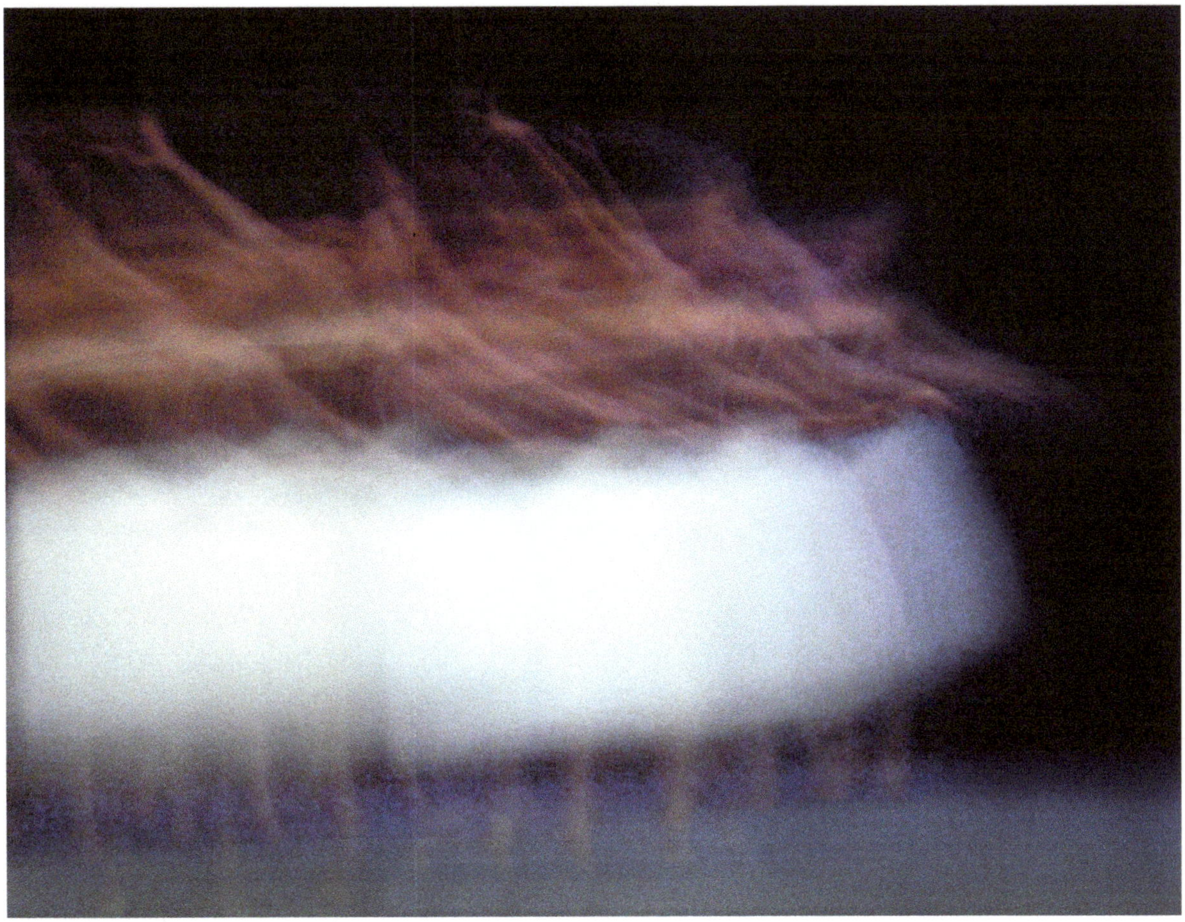

Uncover your Strengths

The trees stand bare in preparation for winter.

Life is always about losing your leaves,
in order to uncover your greatest strengths.

In the most difficult times,
you must go deep within yourself...

and draw on the nourishment that is
deep in your roots.

Knowing, that you will always be able to
recover from the cold.

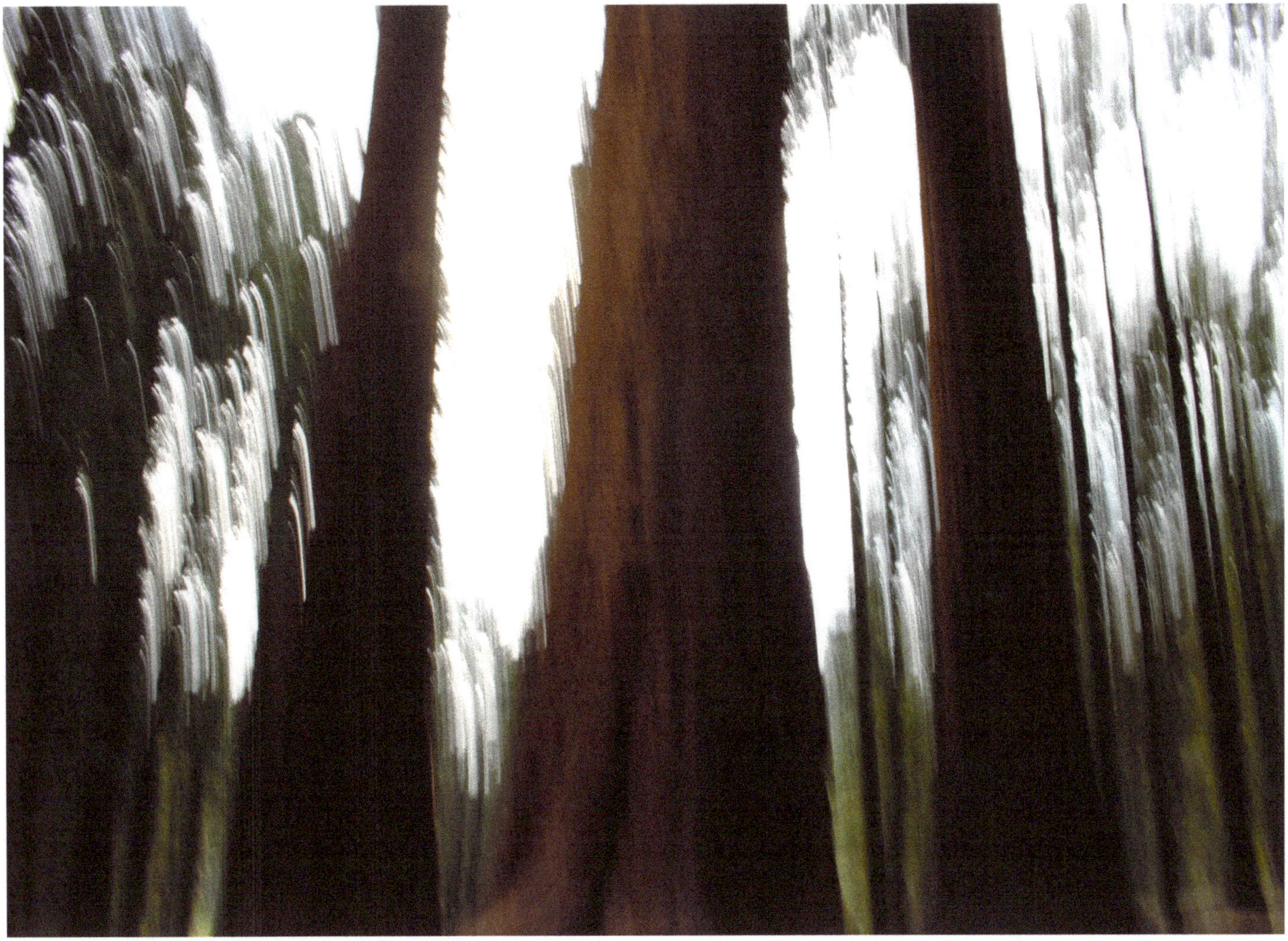

Fruits of Life

The sound of walnuts dropping
from the trees reminds me…

that everything in life has its own special fruit to bear.

But it is only in the releasing of that fruit,
that the true gift is realized.

Raining Leaves

The leaves are floating down
around me like rain.

All around you there is meaning.

As the leaves drop,
they are there to remind you,

that you will always find a way to
rid yourself of what is no longer necessary.

When this happens…
it will free you up to many more possibilities.

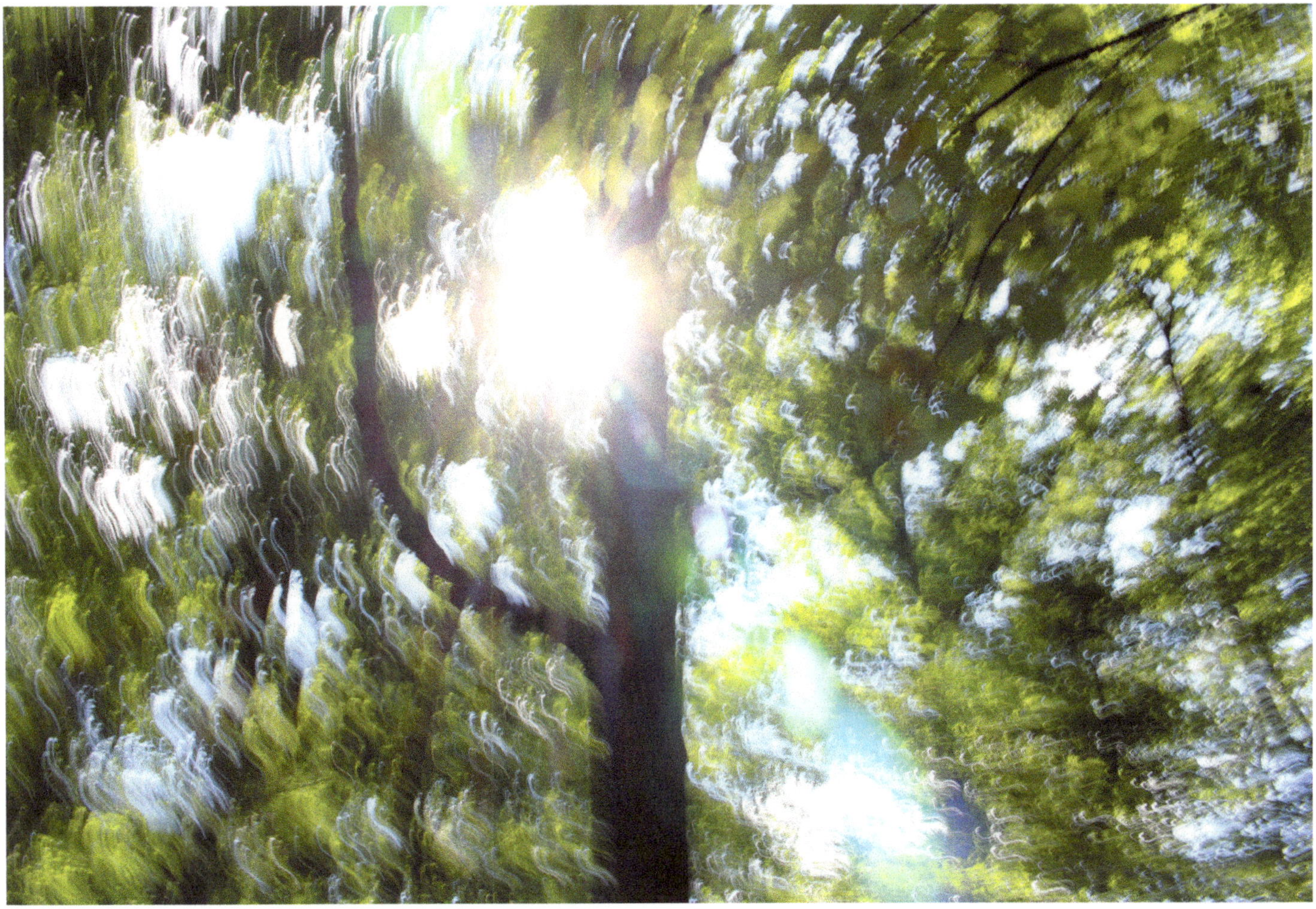

Let Go

Let go, let go, let go.

You cannot force life.
If you are in a river, you cannot swim upstream.

Life is easy when you go with the current.

Free Yourself

Let go of any perceptions
that may be holding you back.

Do not judge.

You will find a way to see,
what you want to see,
if you will get rid of all judgment.

Your mind can create what you want…
if only you can free yourself from judgment.

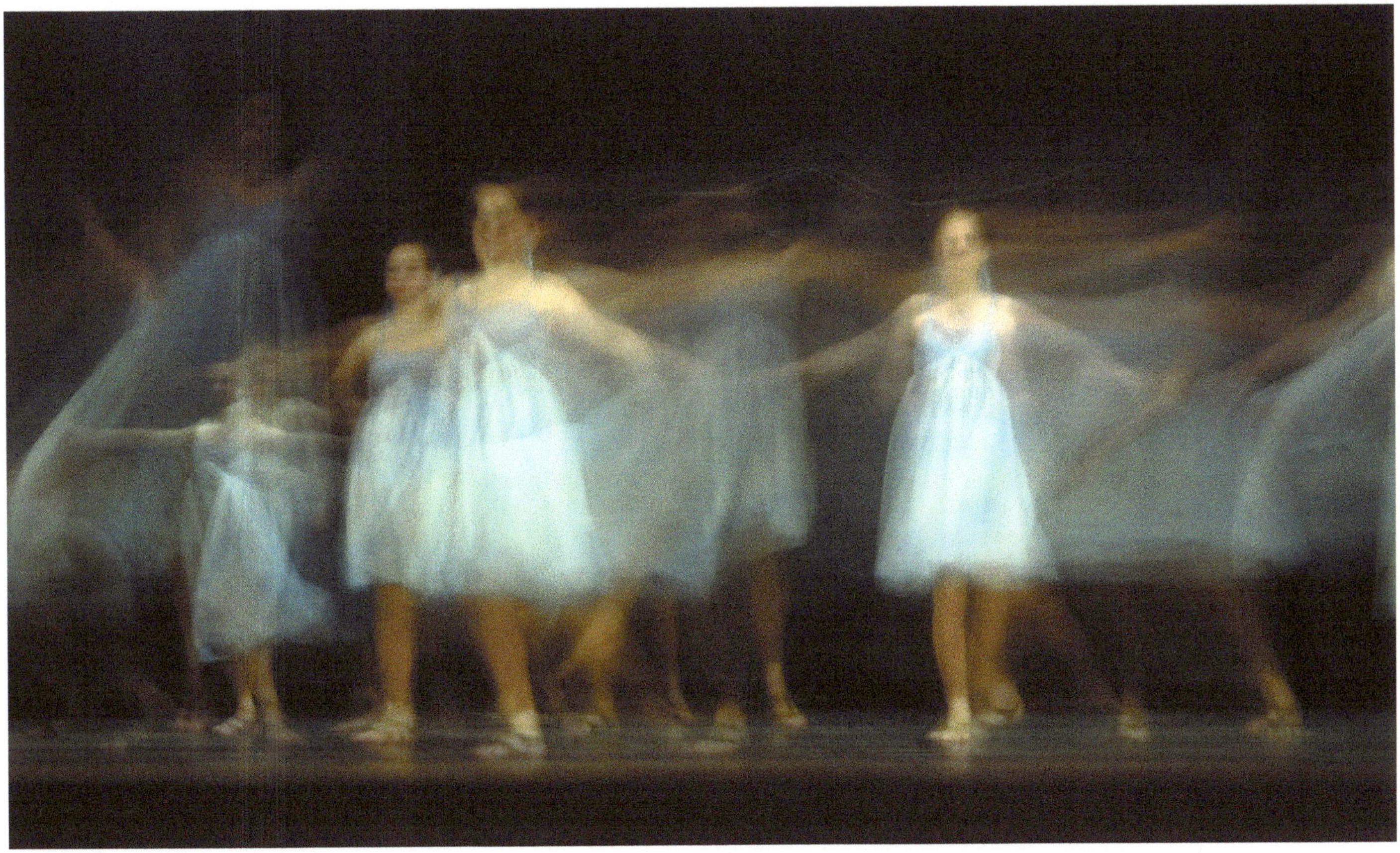

Laugh

Laugh and accept things as they are.
There is humor in all situations.

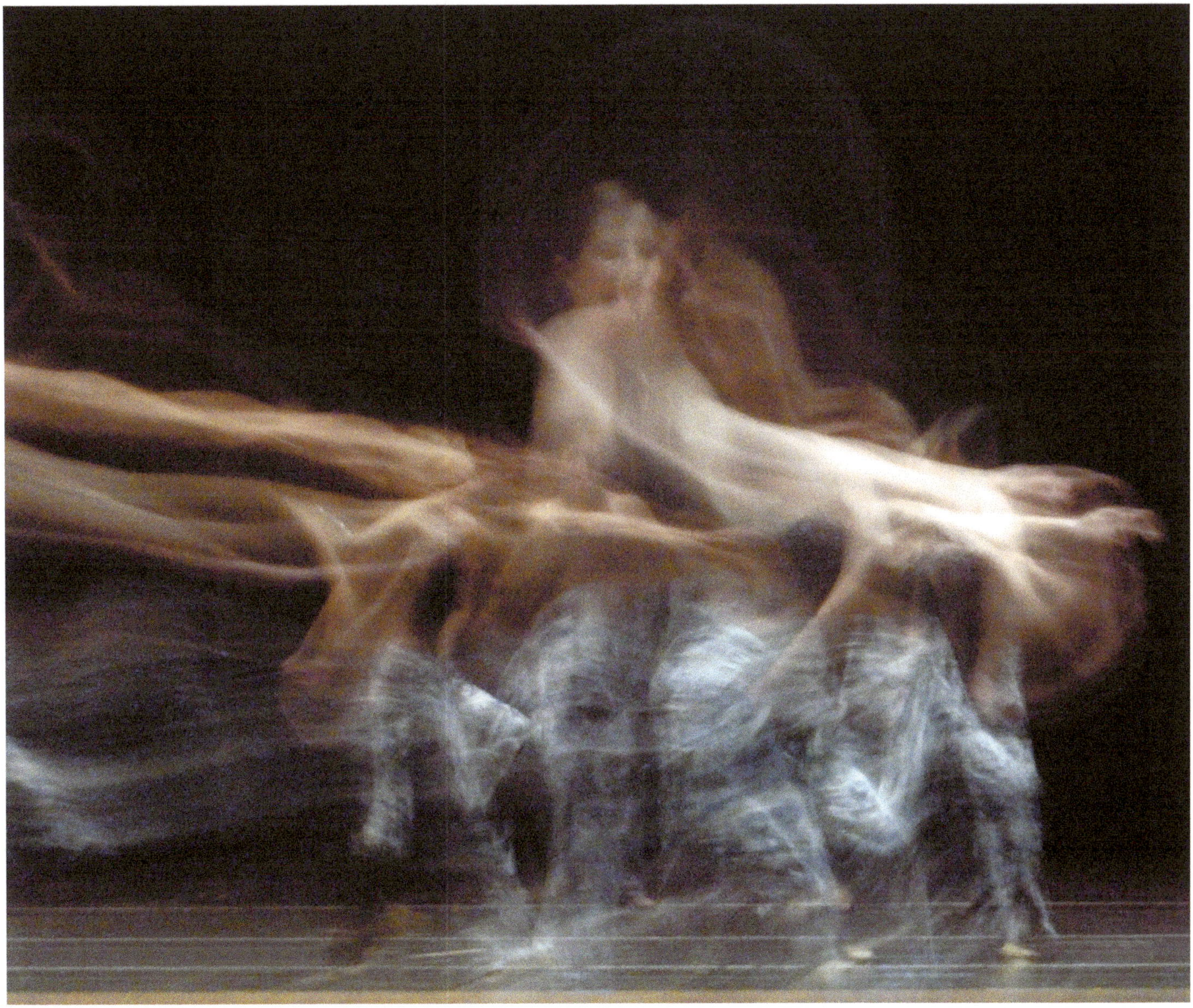

Growth

Growth

The outstretched arms of the trees
twist and turn, welcoming in all of life.

Each leaf opens up like the palm of a hand,
soaking in energy from the sun.

Grounding roots force their way into the earth,
drinking in all that is needed.

Through stillness and patience,
growth is always assured.

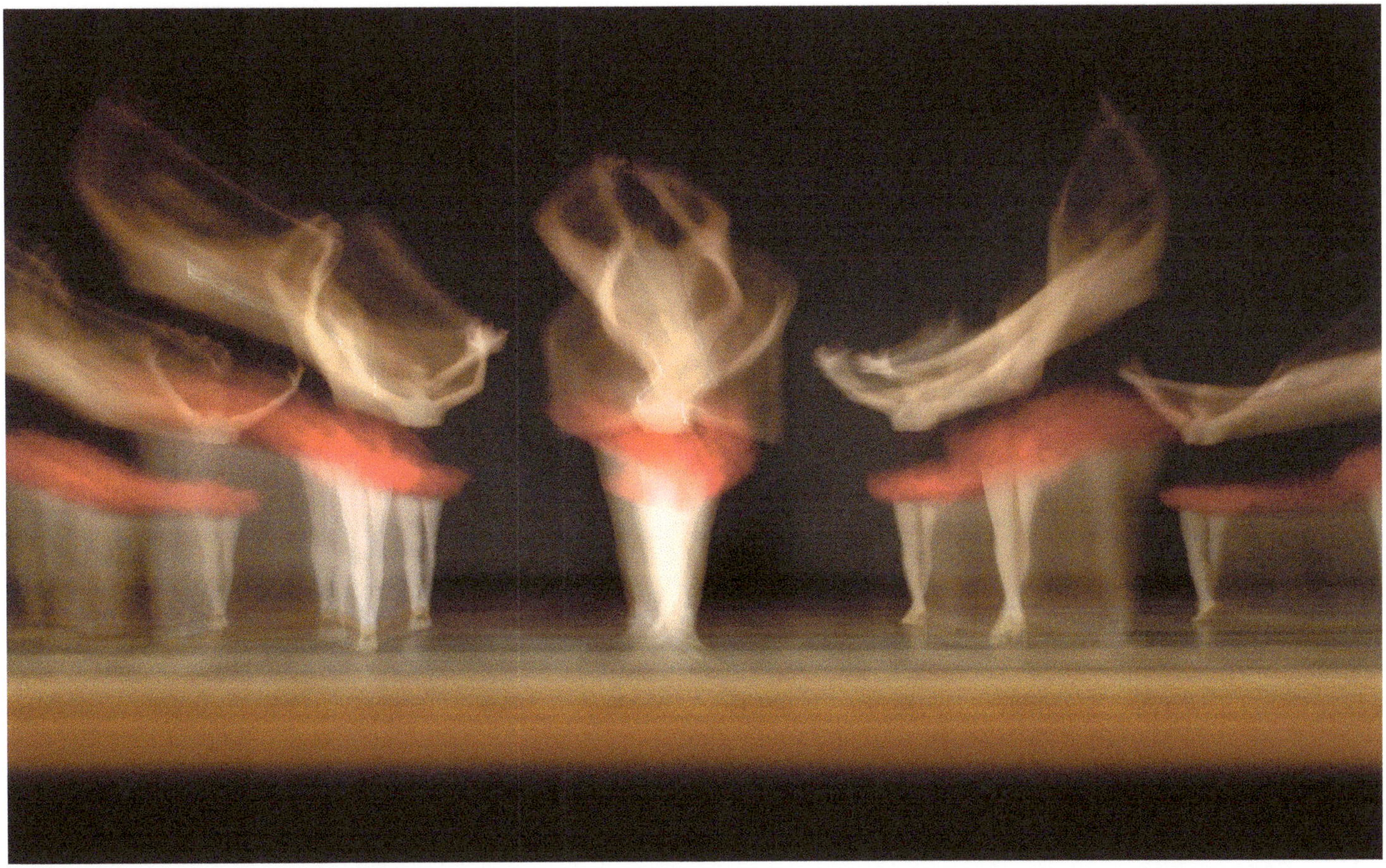

Spirit Reach

Life starts out so innocent and pure.
If only we could hold onto the roots
that keep us so tight.

But the deeper the roots,
the more ground they cover…
the more our Spirit can flourish.

Is that what life is about?
Spreading our Spirit as far as it will reach?

Only then, can we be truly fulfilled?
Only then, can we truly say that we have lived?

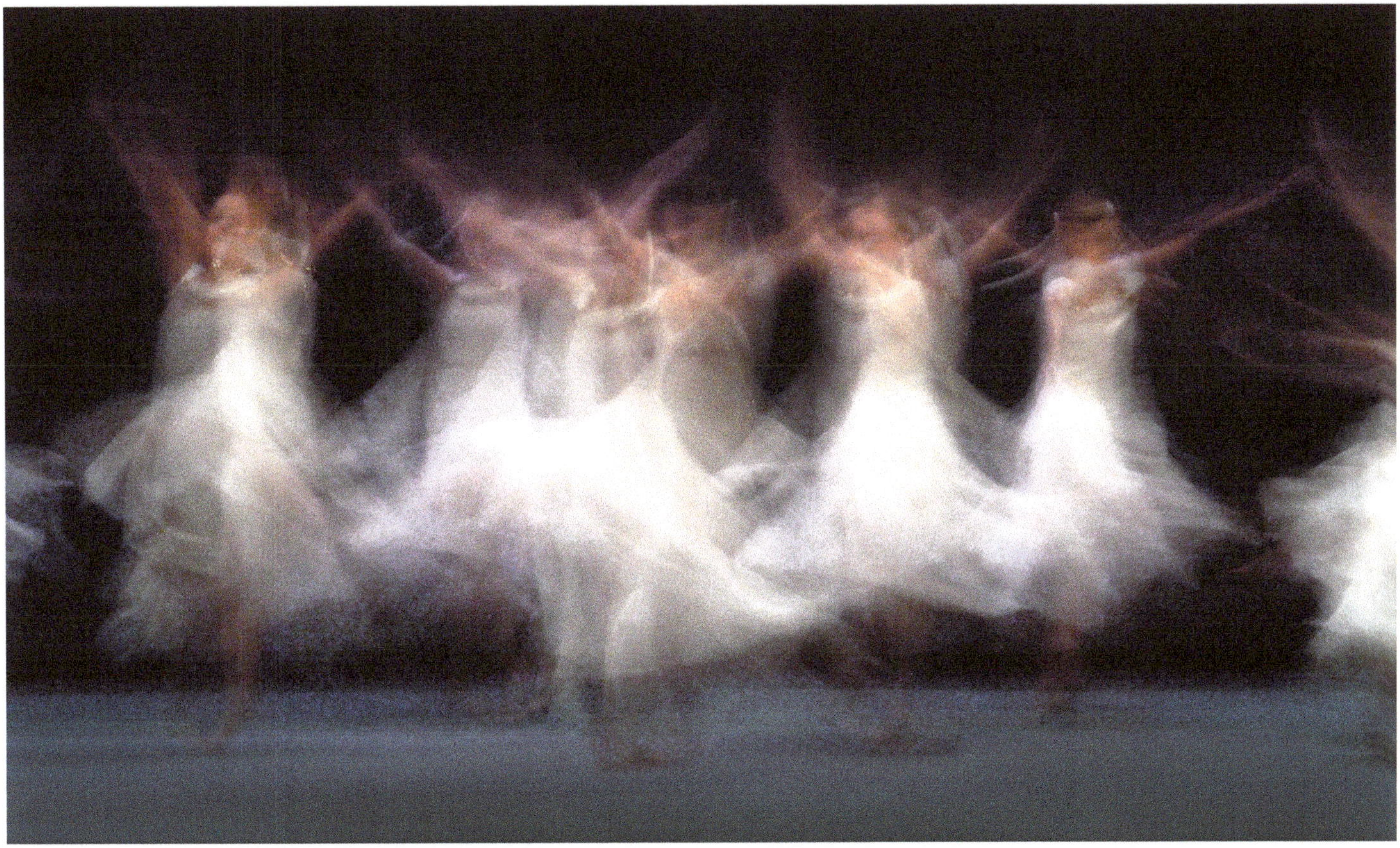

Flow with Life

Growth is always with you.

You have great abilities that need to arise.

One by one you will discover all of your gifts…
and there are many.

Learn to flow with life and you will
always find yourself where you need to be.

Go ahead with ease.

Stop and listen to your heart…
The answers will always be there.

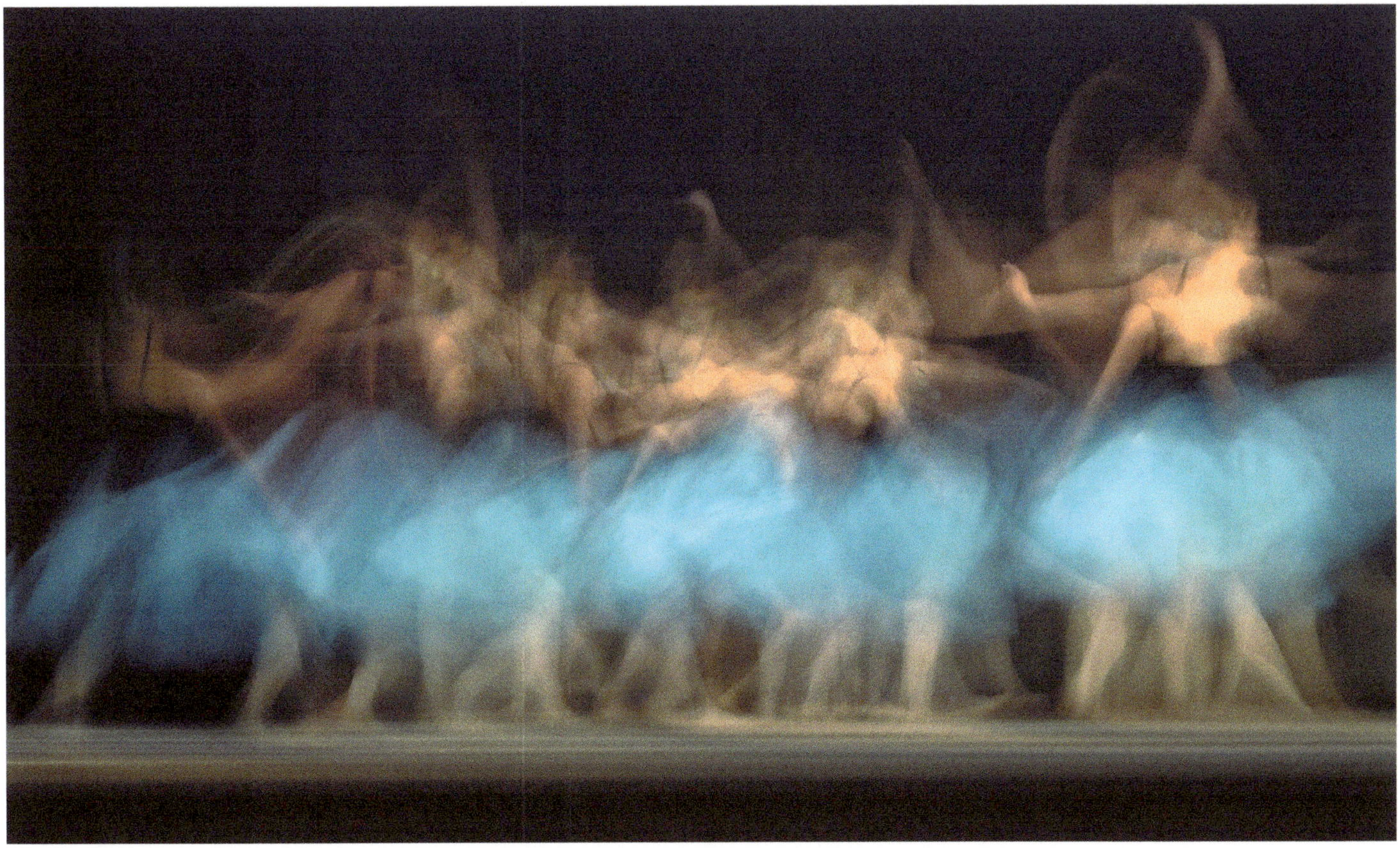

Great Lessons

Be mindful that whatever happens,
is just as it should be.

All will come with ease.

Great Lessons will be taught and learned.
You have gifts to give… Enjoy the process.

Growth is always a learned behavior.
We want to keep ourselves where we are comfortable.

Let go and let the process of life carry you
to your great potential.

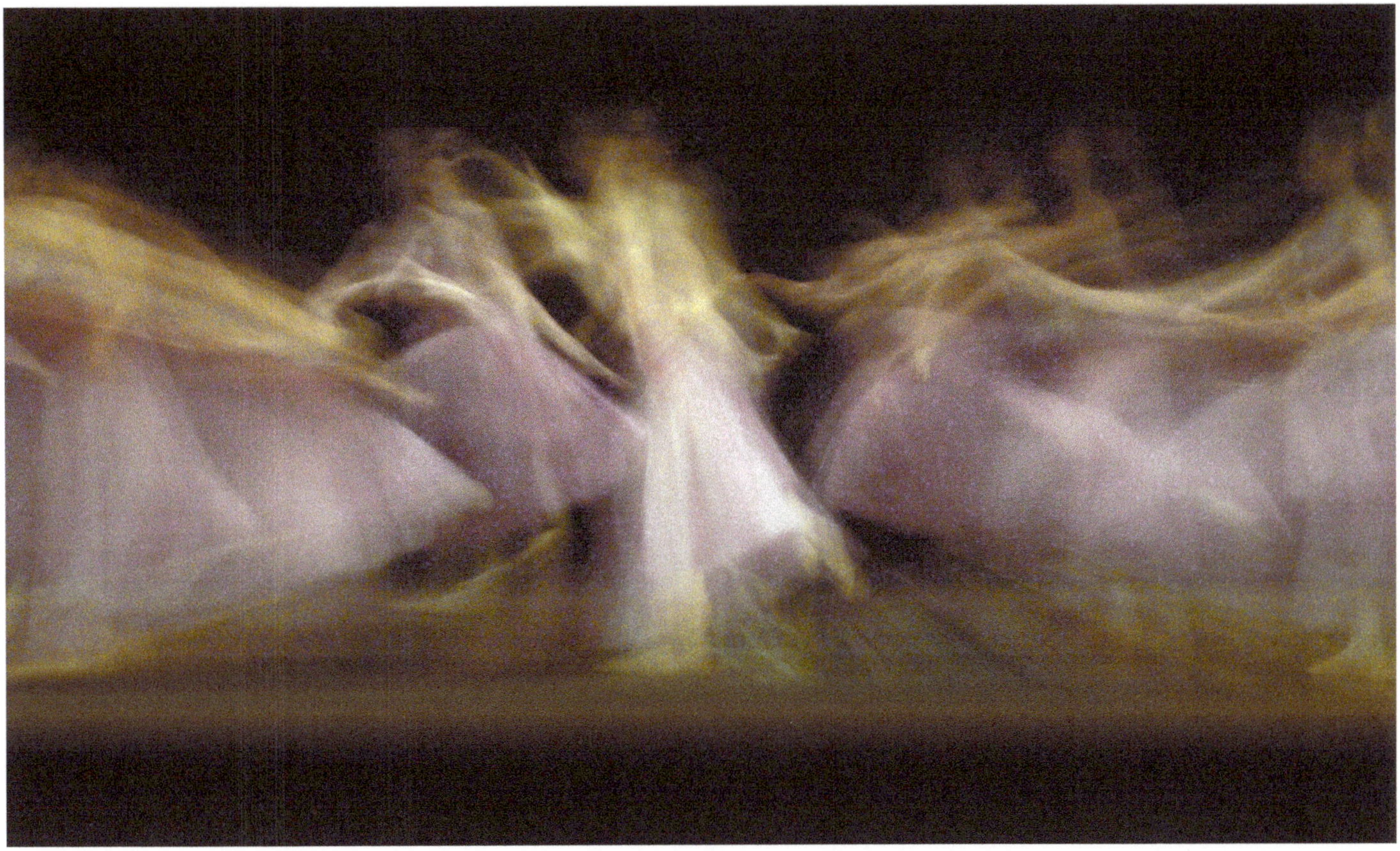

Transition

Transition can be a hard phase of life,
just listen to what your Soul is telling you.

You need to nourish yourself, before you can nourish others.

Take time to reflect on who you are and all will fall into place.

You are special beyond belief
and have great gifts that will inspire many.

Always trust that where you are, is where you need to be.
Keep going and all will be well.

Let go and watch the creativity all around you.
You have the power to create all that is in your space.

Go with the flow.

Stardom is what your birthright holds.
It is a great responsibility and you were chosen wisely.

You are a bright light with gifts that can change the world.

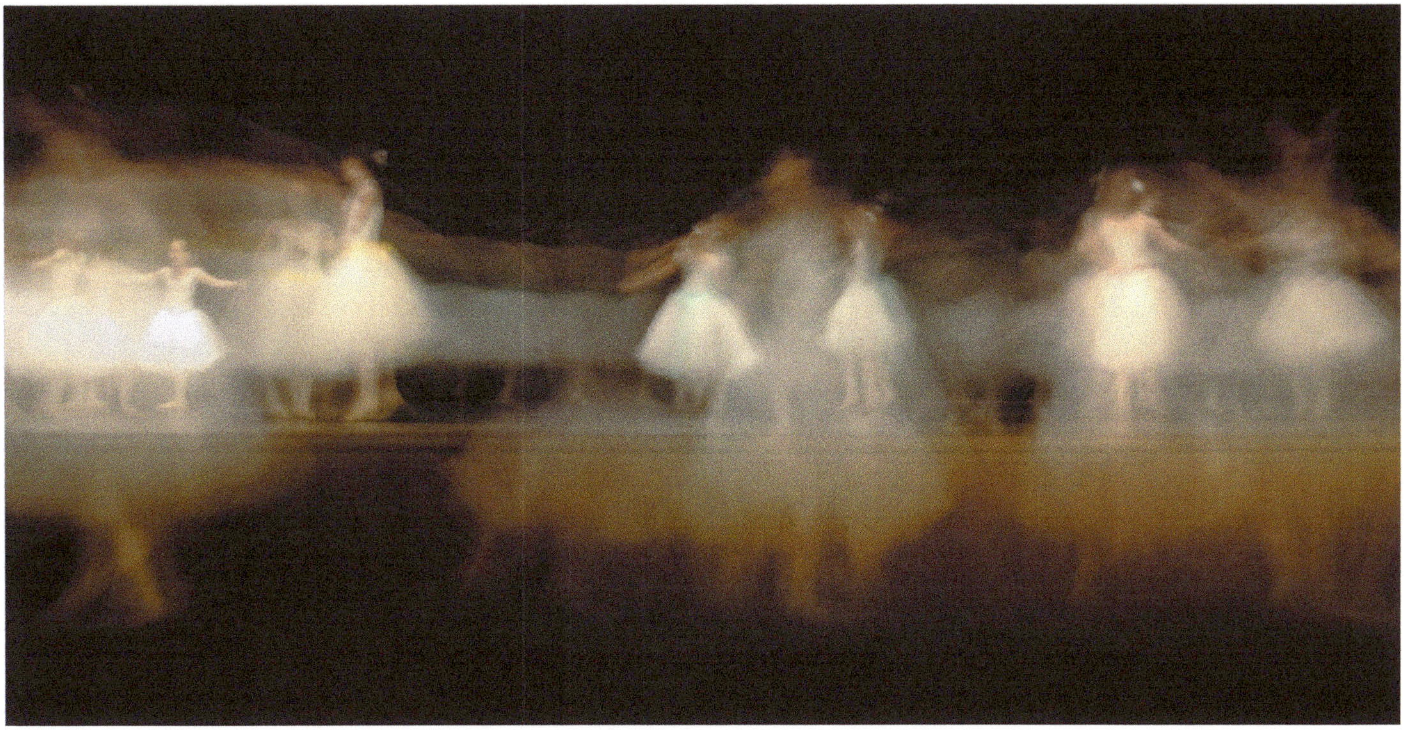

Trust

Life is not always what you think it will be.

Know, that to be flexible...
you have to open your mind.

Forces will always be there to guide you...
You don't have to worry about the future.

Just Trust.
All will be made right, in the right time.

Don't compromise yourself for others...
You need to be healthy to help others.

Move gracefully in the direction you want to go.
Listen to your heart... It will never fail you.

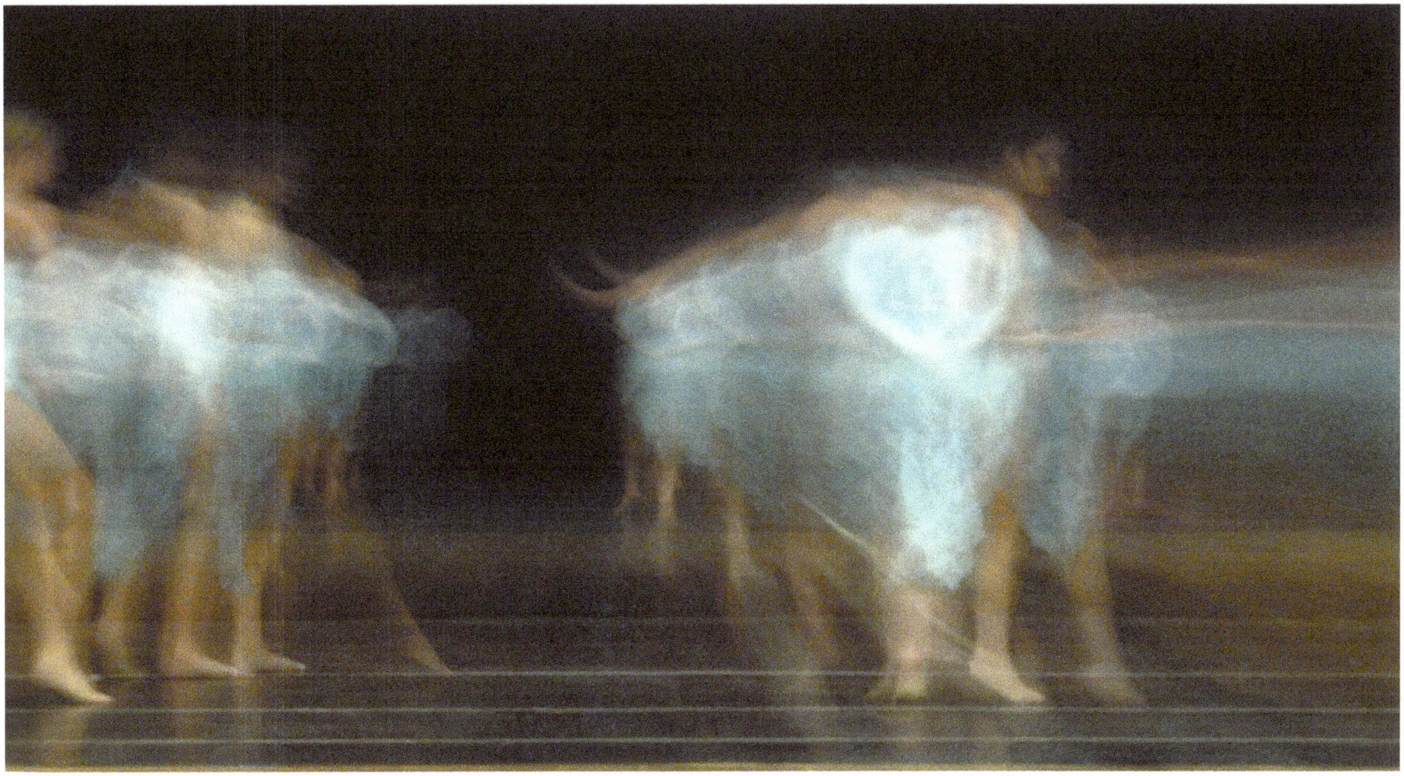

Effort

When the Universe sees we are putting forth effort,
it will be there for us.

When we put forth effort in the world,
all help needed is given.

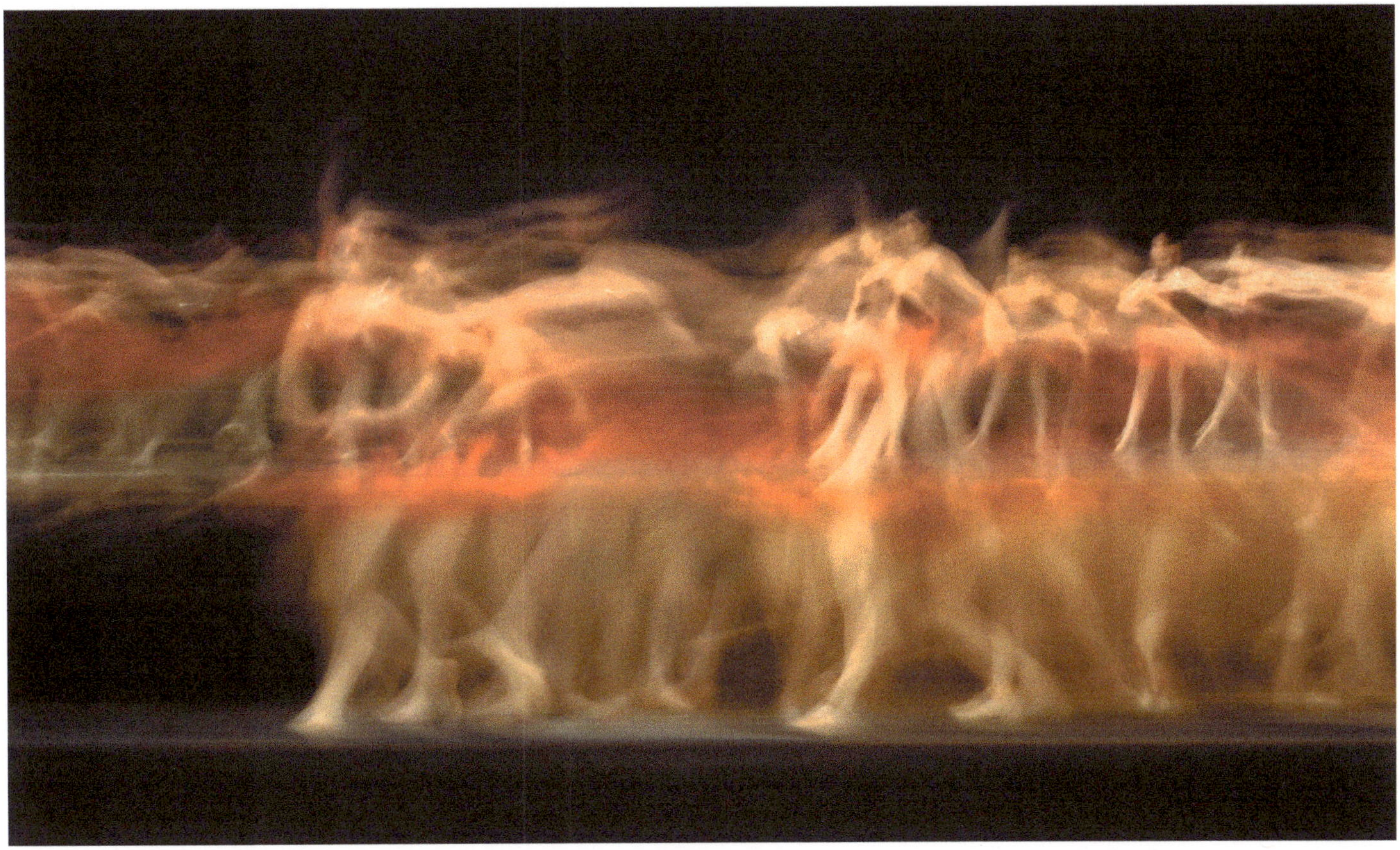

Be in the Moment

Be in the moment.
See things as they are right now.
Notice how you feel.
That is your message.

Step by Step

Take it step by step.
All thoughts will come when needed.

Rituals

Rituals bring the heart and mind
closer together,
when practiced on a regular basis.

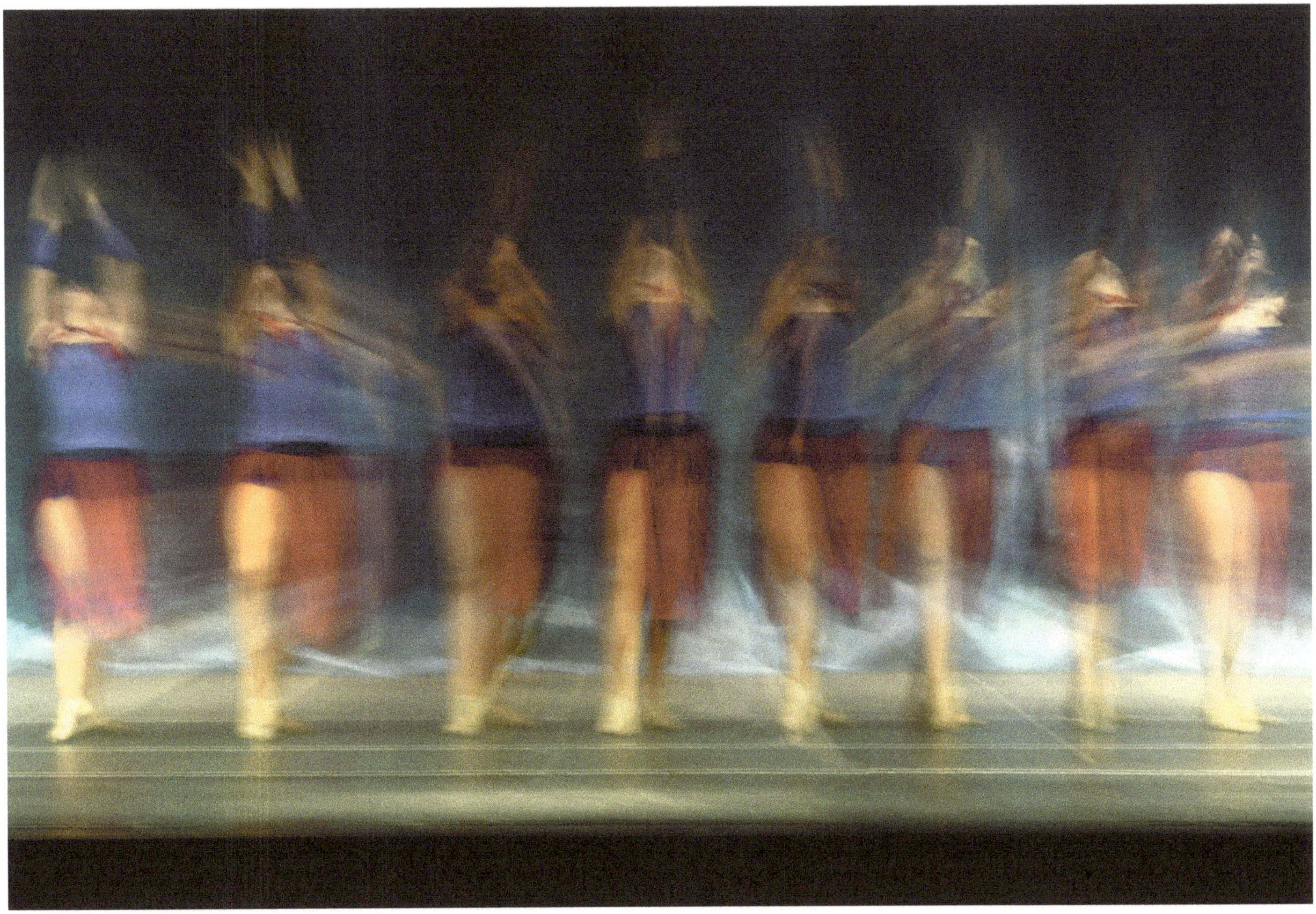

Life Mission

I sit and ponder the great mission in life
that is to be mine.

Go on with ease and know that your mission is great.
You will have everything you need come to you…
when you need it.

Keep going… You cannot stop.

You are powerful beyond belief
and will help many people.

Just trust that the messages we give you are truth.

Do not question your ability…
Everything will come when it needs to.

Trust.

Find time to sit quietly.

Stop thinking.

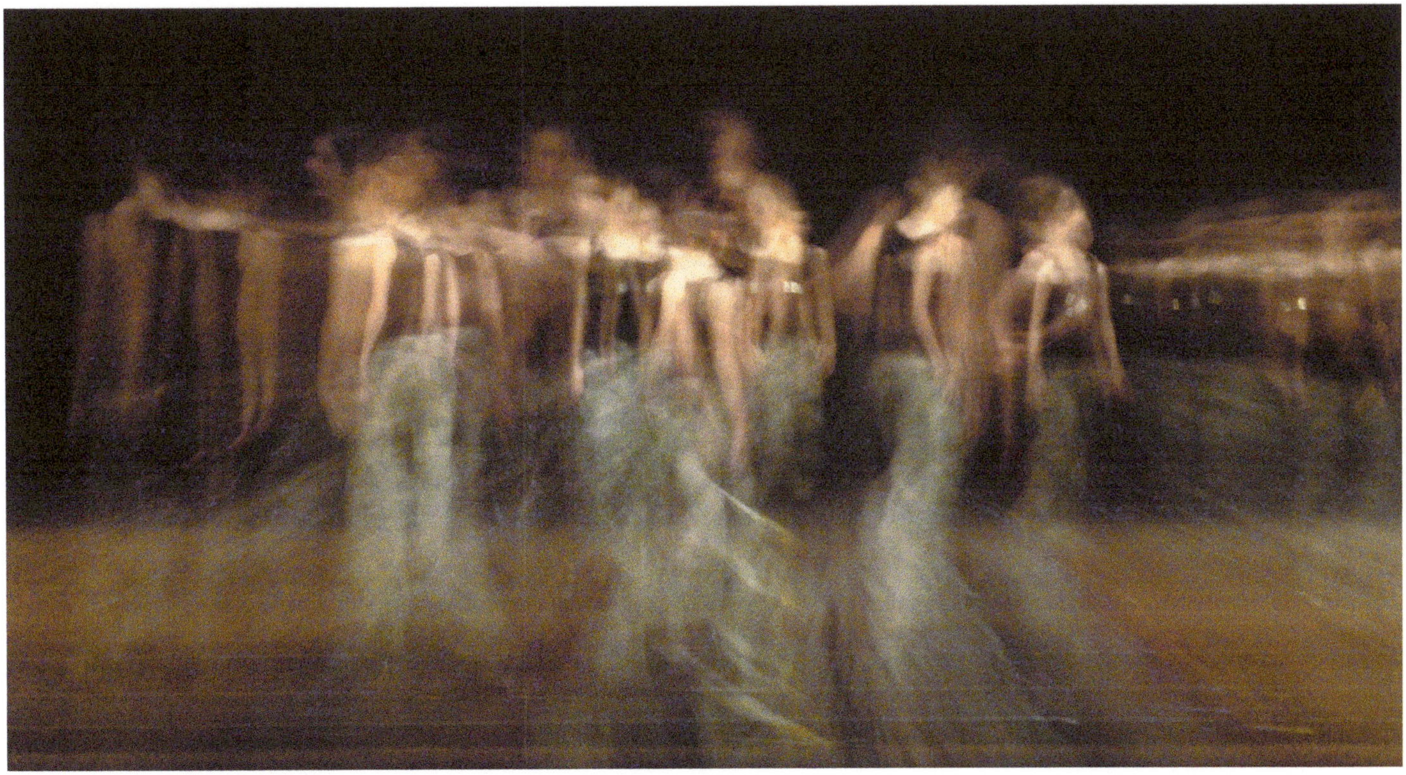

Life Puzzle

With a clear head...
Images of what should be broken,
lie still,
waiting to arise like a puzzle.

Coming together, one by one,
in perfect divine order.

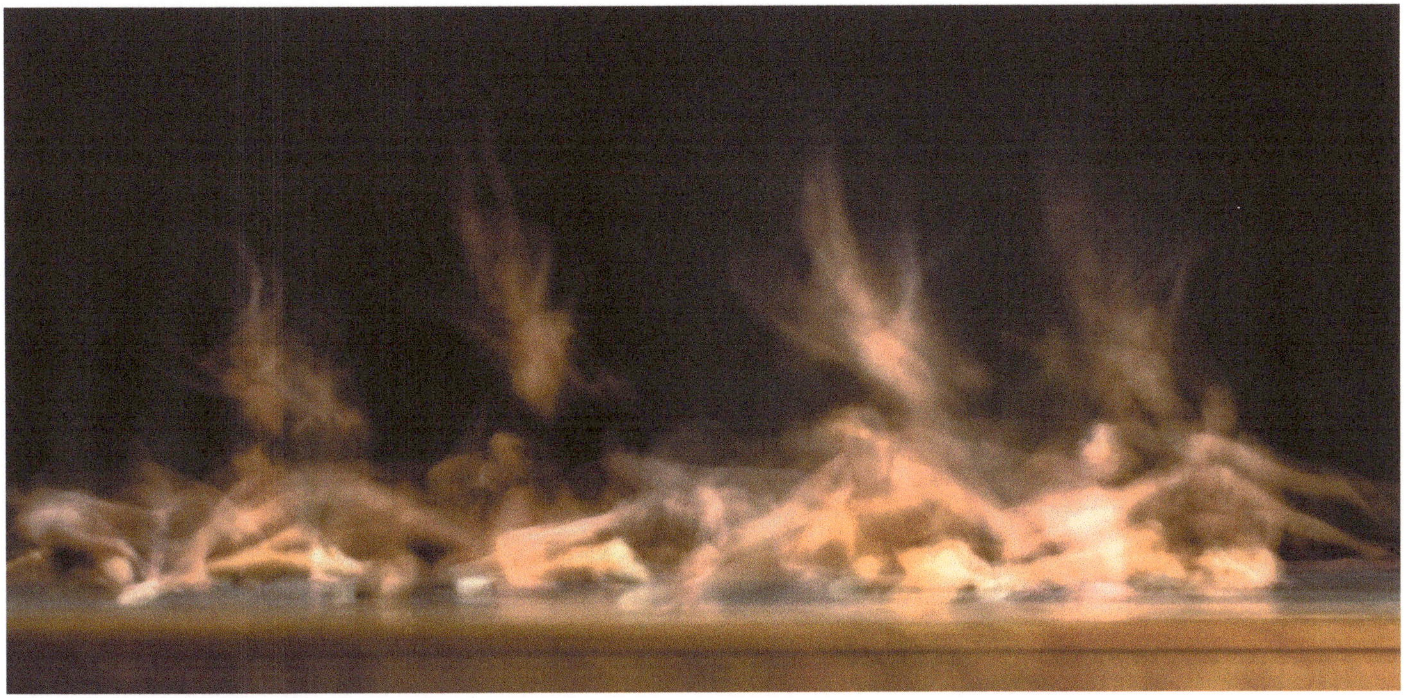

Acknowledgements

John Noble, *my Husband*… Thank you for being an incredible sounding board and voice of reason throughout this new book writing adventure… being my spiritual / life guru... putting up with my late night and early, early morning writing sprees… keeping my mind inspired through our many, many travel adventures... and for always filling me with a great breakfast. ☺

Casey Noble, *my oldest Daughter*… Thank you for being my number one fan… always encouraging me to believe in myself… being so excited about life… always seeing the positive… and for keeping me healthy by opening my mind to new, fun and exciting adventures. ☺

Bailey Noble, *my youngest Daughter*… Thank you for being my soul sister… my teacher… the person I go to for amazing insight on anything from books, to life… and for sharing my spiritual journey, through yoga, meditation and philosophy. ☺

Casey and Bailey, again… my Bright Lights… you both inspire me by the way you live your lives… you are both caring and compassionate… always spreading joy and shining a bright light on everyone you meet!!! ☺

Jetty, *my Dog*… Thank you for being by my side through my entire book journey… always keeping my feet warm under my desk... and for inspiring me with the optimism that only a pet can have. ☺

Josephine Rosenberg, *my Grammy*… Thank you for being my greatest teacher and inspiration. Because of you, I had the best human and spiritual foundation to build the most amazing life possible. I miss you so much!!! ☺

Scott Katsura, *my new Friend*… Thank you for being divinely sent to inspire me to finish my book… helping me navigate the publishing process… offering amazing ideas for my book cover… and for your extraordinary words that now grace the back of my book. ☺

Wayne Dyer, *my Teacher*… Thank you for our long, inspiring talk that we shared many years ago. You unknowingly encouraged me to see the beauty in my photographs, which led me to the beautiful words that now surround them within this book. ☺

Family and Friends… Thank you for shining your light on me… you all inspire me everyday!!! ☺

Thank you Spirit,
for taking me along on this
AMAZING,
Journey to my Soul!!! ☺

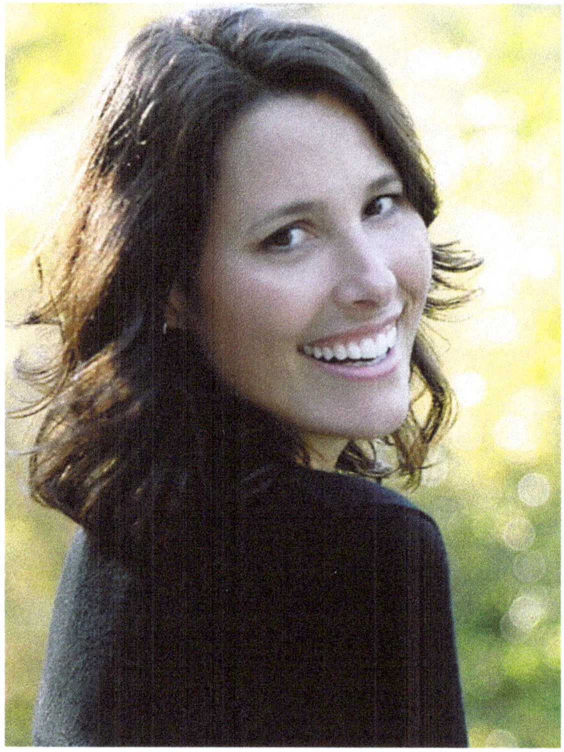

Lynn Noble is happily married, has
two amazing, beautiful daughters and a sweet Golden Retriever.
As a photographer, she has a love of capturing the
"Spirit"... in dance, theatre, people and nature.
As an actress, she has graced the screen in
commercials, television, films and QVC.
Her love of inspiring people has led her to teaching
commercial acting and filmmaking to young adults and children.
Writing is her newest adventure and
"Let the Spirit Move You"
is just the first of many books to follow.
Enjoy!!! ☺